iPhone 8 Ma

Kelly Famorenah

Table of Contents

Introduction

The easy-to-follow steps in this book would help you manage, personalize, and communicate better using your new iPhone 8, and iPhone 8 Plus cell phone optimally.

You would discover how to do everything from the set-up process to customizing the iPhone, as well as amazing Tips & tricks you never would find in the original iPhone manual.

You would discover how to do everything from the set-up process to customizing the iPhone, as well as amazing Tips & tricks you never would find in the original iPhone manual. Among what you would learn are;

- iPhone 8 correct set-up process
- iPhone 8 Plus Features
- How to personalize your iPhone
- How to fix common iPhone 8 problems

- 23 Top iPhone Tips and Tricks

- iPhone 8 Series Security Features

- Apple ID and Face ID Set-up and Tricks

- Apple Face ID Hidden Features

- All iPhone 8 Gestures you should know

- How to Hide SMS notification content display on iPhone screen

- How to use the virtual Home button

...and a lot more.

The easy-to-follow steps in this book would help you manage, personalize, and communicate better using your new iPhone 8, and iPhone 8 Plus cell phone optimally.

There's no better resource around for dummies and seniors such as kids, teens, adolescents, adults, like this guide. It's a must-have manual that every iphone user must-own and also be gifted to friends and family.

Chapter 1

iPhone 8 and 8 Plus: What you Ought to Know

Announced at precisely the same time as the iPhone X, the iPhone 8 and iPhone 8 Plus might appear just a little overshadowed by their fancy new sibling. Sure they don't have all the elegant top features of the iPhone X, but to state that the iPhone 8 and iPhone 8 Plus aren't perfect iPhones and can't keep their own is incorrect.

The Coolest New Top features of the iPhone 8 and iPhone 8 Plus Coming just one single year following the iPhone 7 and iPhone 7 Plus, it might be easy to presume the update to the iPhone 8 and iPhone 8 Plus would be small, even if its a welcomed one. From hook distance, you might even mistake the iPhone 8 for the iPhone 7, but under the display, there are serious improvements.

- **iPhone 8 Processors**

The first among these improvements is the cutting-edge, 64-bit, multicore A11 Bionic processor chip, and an all-new Images Processing Device. These chips deliver major HP for processing- and graphics-intensive jobs. The iPhone 7 series was built around powerful chips; however the A11 Bionic is 25% percent to 70% faster than the iPhone 7's A10 Fusion chip, relating to Apple. *How fast?* In some instances, the A11 is faster than it's predecessors.

The iPhone 8's GPU is approximately 30% faster than the main one in the seven series; that GPU is utilized for the camera and Apple's execution of augmented fact. The camera on the iPhone 8 seems superficially exactly like that on the iPhone 7. It requires 12-megapixel images and catches 4K video, but those specifications don't meet up the iPhone 8's improvements.

- **iPhone 8 Cameras**

The iPhone 8's camera system allows 83% more light into its sensor, leading to better low-light pictures and more true-to-life colors. Around the iPhone 8 Plus, this allows a new Family portrait mode, where the camera senses light and depth as you compose a picture and dynamically adjusts to produce the best-looking image.

Video saving is nicely boosted too. The 8 series can catch 4K video at up to 60 fps (up from 30 fps on the 7) and slow-motion, 240-frame-per-second video in 1080p (in comparison to 120 fps on the 7).

- **Augmented Reality**

The iPhone 8's GPU is also necessary to its Augmented

Reality features. Augmented Fact or AR, combines live data from the web with images of the real-world in front of you (like viewing Pokemon apparently in your living room in Pokemon Go). AR takes a private camera to ensure it works wherever you are and in whatever conditions, and a powerful GPU for merging data, live images, and digital animations. The excess hp under the iPhone 8's hood and cleverness included in its digital cameras make the iPhone 8 suitable to AR.

- **<u>iPhone 8 Design and Wireless Charging</u>**

As the iPhone 8 and iPhone 8 Plus appear to be recent versions of the iPhone, they will vary. Eliminated is the aluminium back, changed with an all-new cup back. And, despite what skeptics might state, it isn't to help Apple get additional money from broken cup sections. It's for providing power.

Thanks to the glass back, the iPhone 8 and iPhone 8 Plus enable inductive charging (also known as *wi-fi charging* despite, you understand, needing a cable). With it, you can neglect plugging in your iPhone to charge it. Just place the iPhone on a radio charging mat, and power moves from a wall structure store through the charging mat in to the phone's electric battery. Predicated on the trusted Qi standard, it will eventually be easy to charge the iPhone 8 at home or on the go in international airports and other locations.

In case your charging mat is linked to power through USB-C, the fast-charging feature provides iPhone 8 a 50% charge in only 30 minutes. iPhone 8 and iPhone 8 Plus Glass back permits inductive charging. It is considerably faster and with more power-efficient CPU. Also with an improved GPU Camera for truer-to-live color catch and allows more light.

The video camera catches 4K at 60 fps.

What Occurred to the iPhone 7S?

Never someone to shy from breaking custom, Apple's skipped the old naming convention that's existed for almost six years. Before, Apple gets the apple iPhone 4 then your iPhone 4S. The iPhone 5, then iPhone 5S. Completely until 2016.

So, following that reasoning, the iPhone 8 should be called the iPhone 7S. Instead, Apple decided to miss an 'S' and go to the next model. In any event, don't go searching for an iPhone 7S; you may never find it.

C h a p t e r   2

How to Set up Your brand-new iPhone 8

For many individuals, the iPhone 8 Series would be radically not the same as the previous iPhone model. Not surprisingly, the iPhone set up process hasn't transformed much. However, you might end up on the familiar ground; you may still find a lot of little things you honestly must do before you switch ON your new phone for the very first time (or soon after that).

Let's check out how to set up your brand-new iPhone 8 the proper way.

Setup iPhone 8 the Correct Way

With iPhone 8, you'll have the ability to take benefit of Apple's Automatic Setup. If you're through a mature iPhone without Face Identification, you would see that Touch ID is entirely gone. (Which means you'll save one face, rather than several.)

If you're a serial upgrader, and you're from the year-old iPhone X, less has changed. But you'll still need to update just as usual.

iPhone 8 Set up: The Fundamentals

Re-download only the applications you would need - That one is crucial. Most of us have so many applications on our iPhones that people do not use; this is the big reason we execute a clean set up, in all honesty. Utilize the App Store application and make sure you're authorized into the Apple accounts. (Touch the tiny icon of the Updates -panel to see which accounts you're logged on to.) Only download applications you've found in the past half a year. Or, be daring: download stuff you utilize regularly. We're prepared to wager it'll be considered a very few.

Set up *DO NOT Disturb* - If you're like ordinary people, you're constantly getting notifications, iMessages, and other types of distractions through to your iPhone. Create *DO NOT Disturb* in the Configurations application (it's in the next section listed below, slightly below *Notifications* and *Control Center*). You'll want to routine it for occasions when you need never to be bothered.

Toggle Alarm to On and then Messages when you want to keep Notifications away from that person. Try 9 p.m. to 8 a.m. when you can.

Pro suggestion: Let some things through if there's an Emergency: Enable Allow Phone calls From your

Favorites and toggle Repeated Phone calls to On. iOS 13 also enables you to switch on *DO NOT Disturb* at Bedtime, which mutes all notifications and even hides them from the lock screen, and that means you don't get distracted when you take the phone to check the time.

Auto Setup for iPhone 8

Secondly; Auto Setup enables you to duplicate your Apple ID and home Wi-Fi configurations from another device, simply by getting them close collectively.

In case your old iPhone (or iPad) has already been operating iOS 12 or iOS 13, to put it simply the devices next to one another. Then follow the prompts to avoid needing to enter your Apple ID and Wi-Fi passwords; this makes the original iPhone set up much smoother.

Set up a fresh iPhone 8 from Scratch

The guide below assumes you're establishing your brand-new iPhone from scratch. If you don't wish to accomplish that, you'll need to acquire any of the other iPhone manuals for beginners that I have written.

Restoring from a back-up of Your old iPhone

It's probably that you'll be restoring your brand-new iPhone from a back-up of your present iPhone. If that's so, then you merely want to do a couple of things:

- Be sure you come with an up-to-date backup.

- Use Apple's new Auto Setup feature to get you started truly.

The first thing is as simple as going to the iCloud configurations on your iPhone, and looking at that, they're surely is a recent automated back-up. If not, do one by hand. Head to *Configurations > Your Name > iCloud > iCloud Back-up and tap **BACKUP Now**. Wait around until it is done.

Set up Face ID

Face ID is much simpler to use than Touch ID, and it's own also simpler to create. Instead of needing to teach your iPhone with your fingerprints, one at a time, you simply check out the camera, and that's almost it.

To create Face ID on your iPhone, do the next when prompted through the preliminary iPhone setup. (If you'd like to begin over with a phone you set up previously, check out *Settings > Face ID & Passcode, and type in your password, to begin.*)

Establishing Face ID is similar to the compass calibration your iPhone enables you to do from time to time when you use the Maps app. Only rather than rolling the iPhone around, you roll your head.

You'll need to do two scans, and then the iPhone 8 would have your 3D head stored in its Secure Enclave, inaccessible to anything - even to iOS itself (despite some clickbait "news" stories).

Now, still, in Settings/*Configurations* > *Face ID & Passcode*, you can pick which features to use with Face ID, as everyone else did with *Touch ID*.

If you regularly sport another appearance - you're a clown, a doctor, an impersonator, or something similar - then additionally, you should create another appearance.

Just tap the button in the facial ID settings to set this up.

Create iPhone Email

- *Add your email accounts* - Whether you utilize Mail, Perspective, or something similar to Sparrow, you'll want to include your email accounts immediately. For Apple's Email app, touch *Configurations > Accounts & Passwords, then touch Add Accounts.* Choose your email supplier and follow the steps to enter all the knowledge required.

- *See more email preview* - Email lets you start to see the content of a note without starting it. May as well see as a lot of it as you possibly can, right? Utilize Settings > Email and tap on the Preview button. Change your configurations to five lines and get more information from your email messages and never have to get them open up.

- **Established your default accounts** - For reasons unknown, our iOS Email settings always appear to default to a merchant account we never use, like **iCloud**. Tap *Configurations* > *Accounts & Passwords* > *Your email accounts name, and then touch Accounts* > *Email*. Once you reach the depths of the settings, you can touch your preferred email; this would be your address in new mails. (When there is only one address in here, you're all set.) That is also the spot to add some other email addresses associated with your email account.

Advanced iPhone Email tweaks

- **Swipe to control email** - It's much more helpful to

have the ability to swipe your email messages away rather than clicking through and tapping on several control keys. Swipe to Archive, so that whenever you swipe that path, you'll have the ability to either quickly save a contact to your Archive. Or, if your email accounts support swiping left as a default Delete action, it'll offer a Garbage icon. Swipe left to Tag as Read, which is a smart way to slam through your electronic mails as you have them. This only impacts your built-in Email application from Apple. Each third-party email customer can do things differently.

- *Add an HTML signature* - A sound email signature really can cause you to look professional, so make sure to include an HTML signature to your email. If you've already got one on the desktop, duplicate and paste the code into contact and ahead to yourself. You'll be able to duplicate and paste it into an Email application (or whichever email supplier you like, if it facilitates it). It could be as easy as textual content formatting tags or as complicated as adding a logo design from a webserver. You should use an iOS application to make one, too; however, they tend to look fairly basic.

Manage Calendars, iCloud, Communications and more

- *Set default Calendar alert times* - Calendar is ideal for alerting you to important occasions, but it's not necessarily at a convenient or useful time. Established the default timing on three types of occasions: Birthdays, Occasions, and All-Day

Occasions, and that means you get reminders when they're helpful. Utilize *Configurations* > *Calendars*. Tap on Default Alert Times and set your Birthday reminders to 1 day before, your Occasions to quarter-hour before (or a period which makes more sense to your mind), and All-Day Occasions on the day of the function (10 a.m.). You'll never miss a meeting again.

- **Background application refresh** - You'll desire to be selective about which applications you desire to be in a position to run in the backdrop, so have a look at the list in *Settings* > *General* > *Background App Refresh*. Toggle Background App Refresh to ON, then toggle OFF all the applications you don't need being able to access anything in the background. When in question, toggle it to OFF and find out if you are slowed up by any applications that require to refresh when you release them. You'll want to allow Background Refresh for Cult of Macintosh Magazine!

Secure Your Web Experience

- *Browser set up* - Surfing the net is filled with forms to complete. Adding your name, address, email, and bank cards may take up a great deal of your power. Make sure to head into Configurations > Browser > AutoFill to create your mobile internet browser the proper way. First, toggle Use Contact Info to On. Then tap on My Info and select the contact you want to use when you encounter form areas in Browser. Toggle

Titles and Passwords on as well, and that means you can save that across appointments to the same website. (This pulls from iCloud Keychain, so make sure to have that allowed, too.)

Toggle *CREDIT CARDS* to On as well, which means you can shop swiftly. (be sure to only use SSL-encrypted websites.)

Pro suggestion: Manage which bank cards your iPhone helps you to save with a tap on BANK CARDS. You can include new cards within, or delete ones that no more work or that you don't want to use via mobile Browser.

The browser in iOS 13 and later version also blocks cross-site monitoring, which are those cookies that follow you around and let online stores place the same advertisements on every subsequent web page you visit. That is On by default, and that means you should not do anything. Just relax and revel in your newfound personal privacy.

iCloud Everywhere

- *iCloud is everything* - There's without a doubt in our thoughts that iCloud is the easiest, optimum solution for keeping all of your stuff supported and safe. Utilize the Configurations > iCloud and be sure to register with your **Apple ID**. You can manage your storage space in here, but make sure to enable all you need immediately. Enable iCloud Drive, Photos, Connections, Reminders, Browser, Records, News, Wallet, Back-up, Keychain and others once you get the iPhone unpacked. You can enable Email and Calendars if you merely use Apple's applications and services; usually, you would keep those toggled OFF.

Services subscription during iPhone setup

- *Enable iCloud Photo Library* - We love the iCloud Photo Library. It maintains your photos and videos securely stored in the cloud and enable you to get full-quality copies of your documents in the event you misplace your originals. iCloud Picture Library depends on your iCloud storage space, if you have many photos, you'll want to bump that up. Utilize Configurations > iCloud > Photos, then toggle iCloud Image Library to On. (Remember that this will switch off My Picture Stream. If you'd like both, you'll need to re-toggle

Image Stream back again to On.)

- *Use iTunes Match* - Sure, Apple Music monitors all the music data files on your devices, but if you delete them from your iPhone and don't have a back-up elsewhere, you're heading to have to stay for whatever quality Apple Music will provide you with when you listen. If you wish to maintain your full-resolution music documents supported to the cloud, use iTunes Match.

You get all of your music files matched up or published to iCloud in the best bitrate possible. After that, you can stream or download the music to any device provided your iTunes Match membership is intact. Never be without your music (or have an over-filled iPhone) again.

Go to *Configurations > Music*. Then touch on Sign up to iTunes Match to understand this valuable service allowed on your brand-new iPhone.

More iPhone set up Tweaks

- ***Extend your Auto-Lock*** - Let's face it. The default two minutes you get for the Volume of time your iPhone would remain on without turning off its screen may keep the battery higher much longer, but it's insufficient for anybody during regular use. Utilize Configurations, General, Auto-Lock to create this to the whole five minutes, which means you can stop tapping your screen at all times to keep it awake.

- ***Get texts everywhere*** - You can enable your Mac

PC or iPad to get texts from your iPhone, provided you've set up iMessage to them (Settings, Text messages, toggle iMessage to ON on any iOS device, Messages Preferences on your Mac). Ensure that your other device is close by when you utilize Settings on your iPhone, then touch Messages > TEXT Forwarding. Any devices available will arrive on the list. Toggle your Mac or iPad to On, and then check the prospective device for a code. Enter that code into your iPhone. Now all of your devices are certain to get not only iMessages but also texts from those not using iMessage.

- ***Equalize your tunes*** - Start the EQ in your Music application to be able to hear your preferred jams and never have a trouble with a bluetooth speaker.

Go to Configurations > Music. Once there, touch on EQ and established your iPhone to NIGHT TIME; this will provide you with a great quantity raise for those times where you want to blast *The Clash* while you make a quick supper in the kitchen.

C h a p t e r   3

iPhone 8 - Top Features

After months of rumors, leaking, and lots of speculation, the iPhone 8 has finally been unveiled. This latest flagship smartphone as at 2017 was proven to the world throughout a major keynote at Apple's new HQ in Cupertino the other day. The iPhone 8 and much larger iPhone 8 Plus both add several improvements over their predecessors making them the best Apple smartphones as at now.

Alongside the iPhone 8, the united states technology also largely revealed its iPhone X that includes a new design with a display that covers the whole front of these devices. However, with a £999 price, and a release time of November 2018, the iPhone X would be out.

1. **Wireless Charging**

Apple has included wifi charging on its latest smartphone; this means it can get a fill-up by merely being placed on the compatible pad. The iPhone 8 uses the established Qi ecosystem this means it will use most accessories available on the marketplace.

It's well worth noting that Apple doesn't add a charging pad in the package, so you should buy one separately to utilize this new feature. As well as wireless charging, the iPhone 8 can have its battery boosted in super-quick time. A fresh Apple-designed image signal processor provides advanced pixel processing, wide colour capture, faster autofocus in low light and better HDR photos, while a fresh quad-LED True Tone Flash with Decrease Sync leads to more uniformly lit backgrounds and foregrounds.

Apple says that this results in outstanding photos with

vibrant, realistic colors and greater detail. The iPhone 8 Plus retains its dual-lens camera, which, along using its smart zoom and Family portrait Mode, is now able to change the light in pictures.

Portrait Light brings dramatic studio room lights to the iPhone, allowing customers to fully capture stunning portraits with a shallow depth-of-field impact in five different light styles.

2. *A11 Bionic Processor*

Apple's boosting its new processor chip is the quickest ever to be observed within an iPhone. The brand new *A11 Bionic chip* has around 30% faster graphics performance than the prior brains found inside the iPhone 7. If true it's more likely to outperform not only its predecessor but all the latest Google android competition in year 2017 ans early 2018.

3. *New Colors & Cup Design*

Apple has included some new colours on the iPhone 8 with these devices happening sale in space grey, gold, and silver. The iPhone 8 and iPhone 8 Plus also introduce a lovely cup back design and do not worry about any of it breaking as Apple says it is the most durable cup ever in a smartphone.

The finish is manufactured utilizing a seven-layer colour process for precise hue and opacity, delivering a rich depth of colour with a colour-matched aerospace-grade aluminum bezel. Both iPhone 8 and iPhone 8 Plus are also water and dust resistant.

4. *Extra Storage*

There's some good news if you are always working out

of space for storage as Apple has included 64GB as standard. That is double the essential memory on the iPhone 7. Apple, in addition, has ditched the 128GB version with the iPhone 8 featuring 256GB of in-built memory space.

It's also worthy of noting that iOS 11, which launches in a few days, will automatically decrease the size of photos taken on the iPhone's camera, providing users even more extra space.

5 Cool iPhone 8 Features

1. AR - Augmented Reality

This essentially the most impressive new feature of the iPhone 8 because of its ability to perform augmented reality (AR) apps. They don't need multiple digital cameras or sensors to operate. AR applications simply rely on the iPhone 8's back camera.

Since AR technology continues to be relatively new rather than so trusted, the amount of applications using AR is continually increasing. AR offers a new way for individuals to play video games, learn, and shop. It's also useful in everyday living: you may use AR to, for example, measure things easily without a tape measure.

The world-famous furniture merchant IKEA, in addition, has launched its AR app. IKEA Place provides 3D types of IKEA furniture and allows an individual to put them in real-world environments; This implies you don't have to buy a couch or seat and transport to your living room to see whether it suits or not. You can merely use the IKEA application to learn. The application also allows users to buy and order products.

2. Powerful Picture Editing

The iPhone 8 features Apple's powerful new A11 Bionic processor and a better camera. These characteristics make the iPhone 8 a great tool even for professional photographers. The App Store has a great assortment of picture editing apps. Using the right apps, you may make your photos look superb and professional. Among my favourites is **Photofox**. It combines the simpleness of mobile editing and enhancing with the energy and countless top features of desktop apps, such as *Adobe Photoshop.*

The app helps you to edit images in levels, which can be an important function in professional picture editing. Creating unique designs with visual elements is uncomplicated and straightforward. The application is free but contains in-app purchases.

3. *4K Video*

The iPhone 8's camera has become powerful smartphone cameras in the marketplace. Among its most exceptional features is its capability to take 4K video at 60 fps. What's more, the iPhone 8 can also record excellent gradual movement video at 240 fps with 1080p resolution. If you wish to customise your iPhone's camera configurations, go to *Settings > Camera.*

4. *Portraits with Portrait Lighting*

Apple introduced the astonishing Family portrait photo setting in the iPhone 7 Plus. The iPhone 8 Plus will take things to another level with Family portrait Lighting.

In brief, Family portrait photo mode gives you razor-sharp portrait photos of your subject matter with a blurry background. The iPhone 8 Plus, however, provides you the choice of adding special lights like in real a studio room. The very best part is that once you've taken a picture using Portrait mode, you can still change the lighting settings afterwards to make your picture look the same as you want to buy too.

You can customise the light settings of the portrait picture you already took simply by tapping *Edit* on the picture in the Photos app. The Family portrait Lighting wheel should come up, which you can slide to change the image configurations.

5. *Screen Recording*

The brand new iPhones include native screen recording built-in - there's no dependence on third-party apps; this new feature comes in the iPhone's Control Centre, which you can access by swiping up from underneath the screen. The display documenting icon is not in the Control

Centre by default; you will need to add it by heading to

the iPhone's configurations/settings page.

Chapter 4

How to Customize Your iPhone Mobile

Customize iPhone Ringtones & Text message Tones

The ringtones and text tones your iPhone uses to get your attention need not be exactly like everyone else's. You may make all types of changes, including changing the tone, and that means you know who's phoning or texting without even taking a glance at your phone.

- *Change the Default Ringtone*: Your iPhone comes pre-loaded with a large number of ringtones. Change the default ringtone for all those calls to the main one you prefer the better to get notified when you experience a call to arrive. Do this by *heading to Settings -> Noises (Noises & Haptics on some models) -> Ringtone.*

- *Set Person Ringtones*: You can assign a different ringtone for everybody in your connections list. That way, a love track can play whenever your partner calls, and you know it's them before even looking. Do that by heading to *Phone -> Connections -> tapping the individual whose ringtone you want to improve -> Edit -> Ringtone.*

- *Get Full-Screen Photos for Incoming Phone calls*: The incoming call screen does not have to be boring. With this suggestion, you can view a fullscreen picture of the individual calling you. Go to *Mobile phone -> Connections -> touch the individual -> Edit -> Add Picture.*

- *Customize Text Tone*: Like everyone else can customize the ringtones that play for calls, you can customize the appearance like video when you get texts. Go to *Configurations -> Seems (Noises & Haptics on some models) -> Text message Tone.*

TIPS: You're not limited by the band and text tone that include the iPhone. You can purchase ringtones from Apple, and some applications help you create your tone.

Other iPhone Customization Options

Here's an assortment of a few of our other favorite ways to customize our iPhones.

- *Delete Pre-Installed Apps*: Got a couple of applications pre-installed on your iPhone you don't use? You can delete them (well, the majority of them, anyhow)! Just use the typical way to delete apps: Touch and keep until they tremble, then tap the x on the application icon.

- ***Customize Control Center***: Control Center has a lot more options than are apparent initially. Customize Control Center to get just the group of tools you want to use. Head to *Settings -> Control Center -> Customize Settings.*

- ***Install your preferred Keyboard***: The iPhone includes an excellent onscreen keypad; nevertheless, you can install third-party keyboards that add cool features, like *Google search, emojis, and GIFs, plus much more.* Get yourself a new keyboard at the App Store, then go to *Settings -> General -> Keyboard -> Keyboards.*

- ***Make Siri a friend***: Choose to have Siri talk with you utilizing a man's tone of voice? It could happen. Head to *Settings -> Siri & Search -> Siri Tone of voice -> Male.* You can even go with different accents if you want.

- ***Change Browser's default search engine***: Have search engines apart from Google that you'd like to use? Make it the default for those queries in Browser. Head to *Settings -> Browser -> Search Engine and making a fresh selection.*

- ***Make Your Shortcuts***: If you an iPhone 8 or newer version user, you can create all sorts of cool customized gestures and shortcuts for various jobs.

- ***Jailbreak Your Phone***: To obtain the most control over customizing your mobile phone, you can jailbreak it; this gets rid of Apple's settings over certain types of customization. Jailbreaking can cause functional problems and lessen your phone's security, but it can give more control.

Customize iPhone Home Screen

You may take a look at your iPhone home screen more than some other single screen so that it should be set up the way you want it to appear. Below are a few options for customizing your iPhone home screen.

- *Change Your Wallpaper*: You may make the image behind your applications on the home screen just about whatever you want. A favorite picture of your children or spouse or the logo design of your preferred team is a few options. Find the wallpaper settings by heading to *Settings -> Wallpaper -> Select a New Wallpaper*.

- *Use Live or Video Wallpaper*: Want something eye-catching? Use cartoon wallpapers instead. There are a few restrictions, but this is fairly cool. *Head to Settings -> Wallpaper -> Select a New*

Wallpaper -> pick and choose Active or Live.

- **Put Apps into Folders**: Organize your home screen centred on how you utilize applications by grouping them into folders. Begin by gently tapping and securing one application until all your apps begin to tremble. Then pull and drop one application onto another to place those two applications into a folder.

- **Add Extra Webpages of Apps**: All your apps won't need to be about the same home screen. You may make individual "webpages" for different kinds of applications or different users by tapping and keeping applications or folders, then dragging them from the right side of the screen. Browse the *"Creating Web pages on iPhone"* portion of How to Manage Apps on the iPhone Home Screen to get more.

iPhone Customizations that make things Better to see

It isn't always a simple text message or onscreen items on your iPhone, but these customizations make things much simpler to see.

- _**Use Screen Focus**_: Do all the onscreen symbols and text message look a little too small for your eye? Screen Move magnifies your iPhone screen automatically. To utilize this option, go to _Settings -> Screen & Brightness -> View -> Zoomed -> Collection._

- _**Change Font Size**_: The default font size on your iPhone may be a little small for your eye; nevertheless, you can raise it to make reading convenient. Head to _Settings -> General ->_

Availability -> Larger Text message -> move the slider to On/green -> change the slider below.

- ***Use Dark mode***: If the shiny colors of the iPhone screen strain your eye, you may choose to use Dark Setting, which inverts shiny colors to darker ones. Find the essential Dark settings in *Configurations -> General -> Convenience -> Screen Accommodations -> Invert Colors.*

Customize iPhone Lock Screen

Like everyone else, you can customize your home screen; you can customize the iPhone lock screen, too. In this manner, you have control over the very first thing you see each time you wake up your phone.

- ***Customize Lock Screen Wallpaper***: Exactly like on the home screen, you can transform your iPhone lock screen wallpaper to employ a picture, computer animation, or video. Browse the link within the last section for details.

- *Create a Stronger Passcode*: The much longer your passcode, the harder it is to break right into your iPhone (you are utilizing a passcode, right?). The default passcode is 4 or 6 character types (depending on your iOS version); nevertheless, you make it much longer and stronger. *Head to Settings -> Face ID (or Touch ID) & Passcode -> Change Passcode and following an instructions.*

- *Get Suggestions from Siri*: Siri can learn your practices, preferences, passions, and location and then use that information to suggest content for you. Control what Siri suggests by heading to *Configurations -> Siri & Search -> Siri*

Recommendations and setting the things you want to use to On/green.

Customize iPhone Notifications

Your iPhone helpfully notifies you to understand when you have calls, text messages, emails, and other bits of information that may interest you. But those notifications can be irritating. Customize how you get notifications with these pointers.

- ***Choose Your Notification Style***: The iPhone enables you to choose lots of notification styles, from simple pop-ups to a mixture of sound and text messages, and more. Find the notification options in *Settings -> Notifications -> touch the application you want to regulate -> choose Alerts, Banner Style, Noises, and more.*

- ***Group Notifications from the Same App***: Get yourself many notifications from an individual app, but won't need to see each one taking space on your screen? You can group notifications into a *"stack"* that occupies the same space as your notification. Control this on the per-app basis by heading to *Settings -> Notifications -> the application you want to regulate -> Notification Grouping.*

- ***Adobe flashes a Light for Notifications***: Unless you want to try out to get a notification, you may make the camera adobe flashlight instead. It's a delicate, but apparent, option for most situations. Set this up in *Settings -> General -> Convenience -> Hearing -> move the LED Screen for Notifications slider to On/green.*

- ***Get Notification Previews with Face ID***: In case your iPhone has Face ID, you can utilize it to keep the notifications private. This establishing shows a simple headline in notifications; however, when you go through the screen and get identified by Face ID, the notification expands, showing more content. Establish this by going to *Settings -> Notifications -> Show Previews -> When Unlocked.*

TIPS: That link also offers an excellent tip about using Face ID to silent alarms, and notification sounds, i.e., *"Reduce Alarm Volume and Keep Screen Shiny with Attention Awareness."*

- ***Get more information with Notification Center Widgets***: Notification Center not only gathers all your notifications, but it also offers up widgets, mini-versions of applications to enable you to do

things without starting apps whatsoever.

Chapter 5

iPhone Home Button Basics

Possibly the most significant change Apple introduced using its groundbreaking iPhone 8 was removing the home button. Because of the iPhone's debut, the home button has been the only button on leading the phone. It had also been the most crucial button since it was used to come back to the home screen, to gain access to multitasking, to consider screenshots, plus much more.

You can still do all those things on the iPhone 8, but how you need to do them differs. Pressing a button has been changed by a couple of new gestures that result in those familiar functions. Continue reading to learn all the gestures that changed the home button on the iPhone 8.

How to Unlock the iPhone 8

Waking the iPhone 8 from sleep, also called unlocking the phone (never to be puzzled with unlocking it from a phone company), continues to be very easy. Just grab the phone and swipe up from underneath the screen.

What goes on next depends upon your security configurations. Unless you have a passcode, you'll go to the Home screen. If you do have a passcode, Face ID may recognize that person and take you to the home screen. Or, if you have a passcode but avoid Face ID, you would have to enter your code. Regardless of your configurations, unlocking requires a simple swipe.

How to Go back to the Home Screen on iPhone 8

Having a physical Home button, time for the home screen from any application just required pushing a button. Even without that button, though, time for the

Home screen is relatively simple.

Just swipe up an extremely brief distance from underneath the screen. An extended swipe does another thing (check another item to get more on that), but an instant little flick would need you out of any application and back to the Home screen.

How to Open up the iPhone 8 Multitasking View

On previous iPhones, double-clicking the home button raised a multitasking view that enables you to see all open up apps, quickly change to new apps, and easily quit applications that are working.

That same view continues to be on the iPhone 8; nevertheless, you get access to it differently. Swipe up from underneath in regards to a third of just how up the screen. It is just a little hard initially because it's like the shorter swipe that goes to the home screen.

Switching Apps Without Starting Multitasking on iPhone 8

Here's an example in which eliminating the home button presents an entirely new feature; it doesn't can be found on other models. Rather than having to open up the multitasking view from the last item to improve apps, you can change to a new app with only a simple swipe.

At the bottom corners of the screen, about a level with the line at the bottom, swipe still left or right. Doing that would leap you into the next or earlier application from the multitasking view a considerably faster way to go.

Using Reachability on iPhone 8

With ever-bigger screens on iPhones, it could be hard to attain things that are definately not your thumb. The Reachability feature that was first launched on the iPhone 6 series solves that. An instant double-touch of the home button brings the very best of the screen down, so it is simpler to reach.

In the iPhone 8, Reachability continues to be a choice, though it's disabled by default (transform it on by going to _Settings_ -> _General_ -> _Accessibility_ -> _Reachability_). Whether it's on, you can gain access to the feature by swiping down on the screen near the collection in the bottom. That may be just a little hard to understand, and that means you can also swipe along rapidly from the same location.

New Methods to Do Old Jobs: Siri, Apple Pay, and More

You will find loads of other common iPhone features that use the home button. Here's how to execute some of the most typical ones on the iPhone 8:

- **Take Screenshots**: Click on the Side and volume up buttons at exactly the same time.

- **Change Off/Restart**: Press and contain the Part and volume up buttons at exactly the same time.

- **Activate Siri**: Press and contain the Side button.

- **Confirm Apple Pay and iTunes/App Store Buys**: Use Face ID.

Where is Control Center?

If you know your iPhone, you might be wondering about Control Center. This useful group of tools and shortcuts is utilized by swiping up from underneath the screen on other models. Since swiping around underneath of the screen does so a great many other things on the iPhone 8, Control Center is elsewhere upon this model.

To gain access to it, swipe down from the very best right part of the screen (to the right of the notch), and Control Center appears. Touch or swipe the screen again to dismiss it if you are done.

Want a Home Button? Add One Using Software

Wish your iPhone 8 had a Home button? Well, you can't get a hardware button, but there's a way to get one using the software. The AssistiveTouch feature adds an on-screen Home button for individuals with physical conditions that prevent them from easily clicking the home button (or for people that have broken Home buttons). Anyone can change it and use that same software/virtual button.

To allow AssistiveTouch:

- Touch *Settings*.

- Touch *General*.

- Touch *Accessibility*.

- Touch *AssistiveTouch*.

- Move the AssistiveTouch slider to On/green, and a button shows up on the screen that is capable of doing some of the home button's tasks.

Chapter 6

19 Essential iPhone 8 Guideline Tips

It's a shame the iPhone 8 and iPhone 8 Plus didn't include new designs because while they appear to be a somewhat different iPhone 7 and iPhone 7 Plus, there are a few massive improvements under the hood: ridiculously fast processors, better still cameras plus some brilliant new features.

And here we present 19 ways to make your iPhone 8 / 8 Plus experience better still through an array of different tips, methods, and useful alternatives to the things you need to do every day with your handset - use these to become power consumers of your brand-new Apple phone.

1. *Press the keyboard*

The iPhone 8 is big, and the iPhone 8 Plus bigger still. If you're battling to type one-handed, press, and contain the emoji button on the keypad, and you'll see three keypad symbols: a left-hand part keypad, the existing standard keypad, and a right-hand aspect keypad. Choose either left or to squish the keypad to that part for easier keying in.

2. *Customize Control Center*

The redesigned Control Center is a lot handier than before, and you may make it handier by changing its material in *Settings > Control Center > Customize Settings*. You'll find some interesting options within, like the option to include screen documenting or control your Apple Television.

3. *Drag and Drop*

iPhones haven't yet got the energy to drag and drop

between apps, nevertheless, you can now drag and drop inside Apple's applications - and that means you can drag a connection in an Email into a fresh message, move text in one Note to some other, etc. In Records, for example, you work in scenery mode and drag a graphic or textual content selection out, and on the notice you want to drop it into; after that get note opens, and you will move your stop of textual content or image to its desired location. In the Documents application you can move items over folders to move them.

4. *Check out QR codes*

Apple is very late to the QR code party; nevertheless, you can now check out QR rules from within the Camera app. It'll automatically notice that it's taking a look at a QR code and can then allow you to open up the hyperlink in Safari, hook up to the Wi-Fi network, or do other things the code was created to do.

5. *Make Communications Messier, or Mute them*

You will find new effects in Messages: to see them, hold down the Send icon, and tap Screen. You can mute discussions in Communications now too: swipe still left on a discussion and tap Cover Alerts.

6. *Loop Your Live Photos*

Live Photos are lots of fun, and they're even more pleasurable on the iPhone 8 and iPhone 8 Plus: swipe the picture up to start to see the effects options, which allow you to loop or bounce your Live Photo, or apply a long-exposure effect.

7. *A Record at any Resolution*

The camera in the iPhone 8 and 8 Plus shoots 4K at 30 fps by default, nevertheless, you can modify that in

Settings > *Camera* > *Record Video* to improve the speed to 60fps, drop it to 24fps or use a lesser resolution such as 1080p or 720p HD. Normally, the bigger the quality and framework rate, the greater space you'll need to store your video.

8. *Charge without Cables*

You might have seen that both iPhone 8 and the iPhone 8 Plus support the Qi charging standard, so they'll use any Qi-compatible pad, like the pads and charging-enabled furniture IKEA offers. You can even buy an Apple-approved charging pad from Mophie or Belkin for $59.95 / £54.95 / AU$99.95, with Apple's own AirPower pad coming later this season. It's less fast as charging with a wire, but it's much more convenient and Apple reckons it isn't remote in conditions of speed.

9. *Change Light in Family Portrait Mode*

This only is a plus, and it's one of the headlines top features of the phone. Family portrait setting has new light options that allow you to choose from different studio room light and stage lights, and the email address details are instant - there's some serious digestion making the magic happen so quickly, and the initial data is kept so you can transform your brain later.

10. *Uncover the Power of Sluggish Sync*

Photo benefits will find out about slow sync adobe flash already because it's something many digital cameras can do - it's a means to getting more balanced photos when using display in low light by keeping the shutter open up for longer.

In a standard flash photo, the subject is brightly lit and the background dark, but with decrease sync it's much nearer to what you observe with your eye. You don't should do anything to allow this program - it's just area of the camera.

11. *Enter AR*

The iPhone 8 and 8 Plus cameras have been created for augmented reality (AR) applications because of the high power of the A11 Bionic chip. Yes, other cell phones in the number can do the same, but you will get the best experience on the latest handsets. It's lots of fun, and a thrilling glimpse into the future, whether you are looking at IKEA furniture overlaid on your living room or Thomas & Friends Minis on the espresso table.

12. *Change the Picture Format*

iOS 11 introduced a fresh, a lot more efficient extendable for photos called HEIF, and it's the default format.

However, if you would like to store photos in the less effective but more broadly backed JPEG format, you can transform the default in *Configurations > Camera > Types*.

You can do the same with video, changing from HEVC to H.264 as the default. Don't be concerned about carrying this out if you want to talk about the odd picture. When you talk about iOS, it automatically changes from the high-efficiency format to JPEG or H.264.

13. *Share Your Storage*

This is a large one for families: now you can share your iCloud space with the family. for example, we've got a 2TB plan that people share with the youngsters. You can allow this in *Settings > iCloud > Manage Storage*. Don't get worried; your key iCloud documents aren't distributed, just your space for storage.

14. *Don't Crash the Automobile*

Using your telephone while travelling is, of course, stupid and dangerous, but if you're uncertain that you can avoid temptation then allow *DO NOT Disturb* While Traveling in *Settings > DO NOT Disturb.*

The name lets you know what it can, however, not how clever it is: your iPhone can tell how fast you're moving or whether you're linked for an in-car Bluetooth system, and turn the feature on automatically. It won't stop phone calls, and folks can still reach you within an emergency. However, be warned! It'll also do the same on the train, which may be irritating on the commute to work and you're sitting thinking why nobody enjoys you.

15. *Organize Your Files*

The brand new Files app is currently on iPhone, and it's a

useful way of accessing not only iCloud but third-party services such as Dropbox and Google Drive too. However, most file exchanges are still dealt with by the inbuilt 'Talk about' icon in the relevant apps, rather than using Data files, but if you would like to talk about things from Webpages or similar, this is the spot to come.

16. *Toggle True Tone*

The iPhone 8 and 8 Plus get a good feature that once was limited to iPads: True Tone screen, which adjusts the screen color temperature and brightness predicated on the ambient light conditions. In the unlikely event that you don't want the colors to become more realistic on the display screen, you can toggle it in *Settings > Display and Brightness* or by pressing hard on the brightness slider in charge Center, through 3D Touch.

17. *Switch off Auto-Brightness*

If you like to adapt to the display's brightness yourself rather than leaving it to your iPhone's care setting, you'll wish to know the new location of Auto-Brightness - it's been moved out of *Settings > Display & Brightness and today live in Settings > Accessibility > Display Accommodations.*

18. *Plan Emergencies*

The brand new Emergency SOS feature, which you can allow in *Settings > Emergency SOS*, disables **Touch ID** when activated and can automatically call an emergency number or notify named contacts that you'll require assistance. To utilize it, ***press the Power Button five(5) times***.

19. *Get Yourself a Guide*

I have written a lot of books on how to use several

iPhone devices, the titps and tricks needed, ipad guide books and lot more. Many Authors under Engolee Publishing House has written other Guide too. Also; Apple has published a huge iPhone consumer guide for iBooks. It's free, and you could obtain it for additional information.

Chapter 7

iPhone 8 Unique Beginners Tips

We know thousands of individuals just obtained an iPhone 8 when relatives and buddies members upgraded to one of Apple's newer models, so if you're left with one, here are some iPhone 8/8 Plus changes that may not be familiar to you.

(If you've never used iOS 12 before, then you'll find a lot more improvements, but these improvements will be the ones unique to iPhone 8 compared to previous models - but do take a peek through my other hints for some ideas to get more from your brand-new device).

How to Reboot your iPhone

If you've used a youthful model iPhone before getting an

iPhone 8, then you should know that Apple has changed how you Force Restart the unit.

Using the iPhone 8, the Force Restart procedure is really as follows:

- Press and quickly release the *Volume Up* button.

- Immediately press the *Volume Down* button.

- Then press the *Sleep/Wake button* until you start to see the Apple logo.

How to update the software

You should upgrade the program whenever a new version comes, but if you come with an iPhone 8 (or 8 Plus) you will probably still be in a position to upgrade its software in 2022.

How to utilize it one-handed

This won't take long. Keep your iPhone and double-tap the *Home button* to bring your windows down the display screen (you'll know it when you view it) to make things simpler to reach with your thumb. Double-tap again to move it up. And, if you will be keying in one-handed, reach over and press 'n' contain the emoji button the keypad .. on another web page you'll find three keyboards, right, middle and left. Choose the best hand indent if you work with your left hands and the keypad will twist to the left to make it just a little more straightforward to use.

How to charge your iPhone 8 faster

iPhone 8 boasts with a 5-watt charger, but when you can obtain an iPad Pro or USB-C MacBook charger, you can plug your device into those. You'll notice a real improvement in control time when you do. You should strike 50% charge in thirty minutes utilizing a 29W MacBook charger. You can even charge your device wirelessly utilizing a *Qi charger* (nevertheless, you probably understood that).

How to use the improved Family Portrait Mode

If you've used an iPhone 7, you'll know just a little about Family portrait Mode, which gets better still in the XS devices but continues to be great in 8. Family portrait mode was launched with the iPhone 7 Plus, and in iPhone 8 Plus has got the new capability to enable you to change the light effect you utilize once you take the shot.

Just open a Family portrait shot in Photos, tap ***Edit*** and use it as an editing effect. Family portrait mode requires (as the name suggests) better family portrait shots. You can even play with different Family portrait Lighting configurations while taking your shot. (To eliminate the Depth impact, open up the image in Photos in Edit setting and touch the Depth button.)

How to use the Trick cursor

If you are typing or wanting to choose words in editable text, touch, and hang on the keyboard, and you'll suddenly see it has become a cursor to make it much simpler to select words you will need.

Ways to get better Video

Your iPhone 8 catches the video at 4K quality at 30 fps

by default. That's very good quality and should look great, but you can get even higher quality video (though be careful not to fill up your phone with clips you don't need). *Open Settings> Camera> Record Video*, and you may choose to capture your clips at 4K res and a speedy 60fps.

How to handle True Tone

iPhone 8 devices were the first ever to provide True Tone displays. These use light sensors to dynamically change the colour of the display to higher match room lighting, so the colors of what you are looking at on-screen appear to be more consistent; this isn't always what you want, so you can turn this feature off in Control Center by long-pressing the iPhone Brightness button and then switching True Tone off (or on). You can also disable it in *Settings> Display & Brightness>* toggle it to off.

How to use Slow Sync

iPhone 8 series devices were the first ever to support Slow Sync, a technology that tries to mitigate the distraction of taking a graphic using the flash and also attempts to lessen that weird effect that makes the primary item in your image appear all bleached out while the background to look darker.

This feature functions by slowing the shutter speed while making the flash moment faster; this implies the backdrop should look brighter and the adobe flash distraction should be reduced.

The result? Better photos when working with display, even of moving items. What you ought to do? Nothing at all, it's built-in.

CHAPTER 8

Restoring iPhone 8 Backup from iCloud and iTunes

There is no need connecting your brand-new iPhone 8 Series (iPhone 8 plus) to your personal computer, as long as there is a mobile data connection designed for activation. As you end the set-up wizard, you may navigate back by tapping the back arrow at the top left-hand side of the screen and scroll further to another display by tapping another button at the top right-hand corner.

You can commence by pressing down the power button at the top edge of your brand-new iPhone 8 Series (iPhone 8, iPhone 8 Pro and iPhone 8 Pro Max). You may want to keep it pressed down for about two seconds until you notice a vibration, meaning the iPhone 8 Series (iPhone 8, iPhone 8 Pro and iPhone 8 Pro Max) is booting up.

Once it boots up finally, you can start initial set up by following the processes below;

- Swipe your finger over the display screen to start the set-up wizard.

- Choose the language of preference - English is usually at the top of the list, so there is no problem finding it. However, if you would like to apply a different language, scroll down to look for your desired language, and tap to select the preferred language.

- Choose your country - the *United States,* for instance, which may be close to the top of the list. If otherwise, scroll down the list and select the

United States or any of your choice.

- You need to connect your iPhone 8 Series (iPhone 8 plus) to the internet to start its activation. You can test this via a link with a Wi-Fi network. Locate the name of your available network in the list shown, and then tap on it to select it.

- Enter the Wi-Fi security password (you will generally find this written on your router, which is probably known as the WPA Key, WEP Key, or Password) and select Sign up. A tick indication shows you are connected, and a radio image appears near the top of the screen. The iPhone 8 Series (iPhone 8 plus) would now start activation with Apple automatically. It may take some time!

- In case your iPhone 8 Series (iPhone 8 plus) is a 4G version, you would be requested to check for updated internet configurations after inserting a new Sim card. You can test this anytime, so, for the present time, tap **Continue**.

- Location services would help you with mapping, weather applications, and more, giving you specific information centered wholly on what your location is. Select whether to use location service by tapping allow location services.

- You would now be requested to create **Touch ID,** which is Apple's fingerprint identification. **Touch ID** allows you to unlock your iPhone 8 Series (iPhone 8 plus) with your fingerprint instead of your passcode or security password. To set up Tap Identification, put a finger or your thumb on the home button (but do not press it down!). To by-pass this for the moment, tap *setup Tap Identification later*.

- If you are establishing Touch ID, the tutorial

instruction on the screen will walk you through the set-up process. Put your finger on the home button, then remove it till the iPhone 8 Series (iPhone 8 plus) has properly scanned your fingerprint. Whenever your print is wholly scanned, you would notice a screen letting you know that tap recognition is successful. Tap **Continue**.

- You would be requested to enter a passcode to secure your iPhone 8 Series (iPhone 8 plus). If you create **Touch ID**, you must use a passcode if, in any case, your fingerprint isn't acknowledged. Securing your computer data is an excellent idea, and the iPhone 8 Series (iPhone 8 plus) provides you with several options. Tap password option to choose your lock method.

- You can arrange a Custom Alphanumeric Code (that is a security password that uses characters and figures), a Custom Numeric Code (digit mainly useful, however, you can add as many numbers as you want!) or a 4-Digit Numeric Code (a high old college pin!). In case you didn't install or setup **Touch ID** you may even have an option not to add a Security password. Tap on your selected Security option.

- I would recommend establishing a 4-digit numeric code, or Touch ID for security reasons, but all optional setup is done likewise. Input your selected Security password using the keyboard.

- Verify your Security password by inputting it again. If the Password does not match, you'll be requested to repeat! If indeed they do match, you'll continue to another display automatically.

At this time of the set-up process, you'll be asked

whether you have used an iPhone 8 Series (iPhone 8 plus) before and probably upgrading it, you can restore all of your applications and information from an iCloud or iTunes backup by deciding on the best option. If this is your first iPhone 8 Series (iPhone 8 plus), you would have to get it started as new, yet, in case you are moving from Android to an iPhone 8 Series (iPhone 8 plus), you can transfer all your data by deciding and choosing the choice you want.

How to Move Data From an Android Phone

Apple has made it quite easy to move your data from a Google Android device to your new iPhone 8 Series (iPhone 8 plus). Proceed to the iOS app. I'll direct you about how to use the application to move your data!

- Using the iPhone 8 Series (iPhone 8 plus), if you are on the applications & data screen of the set-up wizard, tap *move data from Google android*.

- Go to the Play Store on your Google android device and download the app recommended by the set-up wizard. When it is installed, open up the app, select **Continue,** and you'll be shown the *Terms & Conditions* to continue.

- On your Android device, tap *Next* to start linking your Devices. On your own iPhone 8 Series (iPhone 8 plus), select *Continue*.

- Your iPhone 8 Series (iPhone 8 plus) would show a 6-digit code that has to be received into the **Google android** device to set the two phones up.

- Your Google android device would screen all the data that'll be moved. By default, all options are ticked - so if there could be something you don't want to move, tap the related collection to deselect it. If you are prepared to continue, tap *Next* on your Google android device.

- As the change progresses, you would notice the iPhone 8 Series (iPhone 8 plus) display screen changes, showing you the position of the info transfer and progress report.

- When the transfer is completed, you would notice a confirmation screen on each device. On your Android Device, select *Done* to shut the app. On your own iPhone 8 Series (iPhone 8 plus), tap *Continue*.

- An *Apple ID* allows you to download apps, supported by your iPhone 8 Series and synchronize data through multiple devices, which makes it an essential account you should have on your iPhone 8 Series! If you have been using an iPhone 7 plus phones previously, or use iTunes to download music to your laptop, then you should have already become an *Apple ID* user. Register with your username and passwords (when you have lost or forgotten your Apple ID or password you will see a link that may help you reset it). If you're not used to iPhone 8 Series (iPhone 8 plus), select doesn't have an Apple ID to create one for free.

- The Terms & Conditions for your iPhone 8 Series (iPhone 8 plus) can be seen. Please go through them (tapping on more to study additional info), so when you are done, tap *Agree*.

- You'll be asked about synchronizing your data with iCloud. That's to ensure bookmarks, connections, and other items of data are supported securely with your other iPhone 8 Series (iPhone 8 plus)'s data. Tap *merge* to permit this or *don't merge* if you'll have a choice to keep your details elsewhere asides iCloud.

- **Apple pay** is Apple's secure payment system that stores encrypted credit or debit card data on your device and making use of your iPhone 8 Series (iPhone 8 plus) also with your fingerprint to make safe transactions online and with other apps. Select *Next* to continue.

- To *feature/add a card*, place it on a set surface and place the iPhone 8 Series (iPhone 8 plus) over it, so the card is put in the camera framework. The credit card info would be scanned automatically, and you would be requested to verify that the details on display correspond with your card. You'll also be asked to enter the *CVV* (safety code) from the personal strip behind the card. If you choose (or the camera cannot recognize your cards), you can enter credit card information by hand by tapping the hyperlink. You could bypass establishing **Apple Pay** by tapping *create later*.

- Another screen discusses the *iCloud keychain*, which is Apple's secure approach to sharing your preserved security password and payment information throughout all your Apple devices. You might use *iCloud security code* to validate your brand-new device and import present data, or you might be asked to continue registering your keychain if it's your first Apple device. In case you don't want to share vital data with other devices, you should go to *avoid iCloud keychain* or *don't restore passwords*.

- If you selected to set up your Apple keychain, you'd be notified to either use a Security password (the same one you'd set up on your iPhone 8 Series (iPhone 8 plus) or produce a different code. If you're making use of your iCloud security code, you should put it on your iPhone 8 Series (iPhone 8 plus) when prompted.

- This would confirm your ID when signing on to an iCloud safety code; a confirmation code would be delivered via SMS. You may want to hyperlink your smartphone text code (if you have never distributed one with Apple already) so that the code may be provided as a text. Then enter this code to your iPhone 8 Series (iPhone 8 plus) if requested, then select *Next.*

- You'll then be asked to create **Siri**. *Siri* is your own digital personal associate, which might search the internet, send communications, and check out data in your device and a lot more, all without having to flick via specific apps. Choose to create Siri by tapping the choice or start Siri later to skip this task for now.

- To set up and create SIRI, you would need to speak several phrases to the iPhone 8 Series (iPhone 8 plus) to review your conversation patterns and identify your voice.

- Once you say every term, a tick would be observed, showing that it's been known and comprehended. Another phrase may indicate that you should read aloud.

- Once you've completed the five phrases, you would notice a display notifying that Siri has been set up correctly. Tap *Continue*.

- The iPhone 8 Series (iPhone 8 plus) display alters the color balance to help make the screen show up naturally under distinctive light conditions. You can switch this off in the screen settings after the iPhone 8 Series (iPhone 8 plus) has completed configuring it. Tap *continue* to continue with the setup.

- Has your iPhone 8 Series (iPhone 8 plus) been restored? Tap begin to transfer your computer data to your brand-new iPhone 8 Series (iPhone 8 plus).

- You'll be prompted to ensure your brand-new iPhone 8 Series (iPhone 8 plus) has enough power to avoid the device turning off in the process of downloading applications and information. Tap *OK* to verify this recommendation.

- You would notice a notification show up on your apps to download in the background.

NB: Setting up any new iPhone model: A similar method, as described above, applies.

How to Restore iPhone 8 Back-up from iCloud or iTunes

If you want to restore your iPhone 8 Series (iPhone 8 plus) from an iTunes back-up, you may want to connect to iCloud and have the latest version of iTunes installed on it. If you are ready to begin this process, tap **restore from iTunes back-up** on your iPhone 8 Series and connect it to your personal computer. Instructions about how to bring back your data can be followed on the laptop screen.

In case your old iPhone model was supported on iCloud, then follow the instructions below to restore your applications & data to your brand-new device:

- Tap *Restore* from iCloud back-up.

- Register with the Apple ID and Password that you applied to your old iPhone. If you fail to recollect the security password, there's a link that may help you reset it.

- The Terms & Conditions screen would show. Tap the links to learn about specific areas in detail. When you are ready to proceed, select **Agree**.

- Your iPhone 8 Series (iPhone 8 plus) would need some moments to create your Apple ID and hook up with the iCloud server.

- You would notice a summary of available backups to download. The most up-to-date backup would be observed at the very top, with almost every other option below it. If you want to restore from a desirable backup, tap the screen for *all backups* to see the available choices.

- Tap on the back-up you want to restore to start installing.

- A progress bar would be shown, providing you with a demo of the advancement of the download. When the restore is completed, the device will restart.

- You would see a notification telling you that your iPhone 8 Series (iPhone 8 plus) is updated effectively. Tap *Continue*.

- To complete the iCloud set up on your recently restored iPhone 8 Series (iPhone 8 plus), you should re-enter your iCloud (Apple ID) password. Enter/review it and then tap *Next*.

- You'll be prompted to upgrade the security information related to your *Apple ID*. Tap on any stage to replace your computer data, or even to bypass this option. If you aren't ready to do this, then tap the *Next* button.

- **Apple pay** is Apple's secure payment system that stores encrypted credit or debit card data on your device and making use of your iPhone 8 Series (iPhone 8 plus) also with your fingerprint to make safe transactions online and with other apps. Select *Next* to continue.

- To *feature/add a card*, place it on a set surface and place the iPhone 8 Series (iPhone 8 plus) over it, so the card is put in the camera framework. The credit card info would be scanned automatically, and you would be requested to verify that the details on display correspond with your card. You'll also be asked to enter the *CVV* (safety code) from the personal strip behind the card. If you choose (or the camera cannot recognize your cards), you can enter credit card information by hand by tapping the hyperlink. You could bypass establishing **Apple Pay** by tapping *create later*.

- Another screen discusses the *iCloud keychain*, which is Apple's secure approach to sharing your preserved security password and payment information throughout all your Apple devices. You might use *iCloud security code* to validate your brand-new device and import present data, or you might be asked to continue registering your keychain if it's your first Apple device. In case you don't want to share vital data with other devices, you should go to *avoid iCloud keychain* or *don't restore passwords*.

- If you selected to set up your Apple keychain, you'll be notified to either uses a Security password (the same one you'd set up on your iPhone 8 Series (iPhone 8 plus)) or provide a different code. If you're making use of your iCloud security code, you should put it on your iPhone 8 Series (iPhone 8 plus) when prompted.

- This would confirm your ID when signing on to an

iCloud safety code; a confirmation code would be delivered via SMS. You may want to hyperlink your smartphone text code (if you have never distributed one with Apple already) so that the code may be provided as a text. Then enter this code to your iPhone 8 Series (iPhone 8 plus) if requested, then select *Next.*

- You'll then be asked to create **Siri**. *Siri* is your own digital personal associate, which might search the internet, send communications, and check out data in your device and a lot more, all without having to flick via specific apps. Choose to create Siri by tapping the choice or start Siri later to skip this task for now.

- To set up and create SIRI, you would need to speak several phrases to the iPhone 8 Series (iPhone 8 plus) to review your conversation patterns and identify your voice.

- Once you say every term, a tick would be observed, showing that it's been known and comprehended. Another phrase may indicate that you should read aloud.

- Once you've completed the five phrases, you would notice a display notifying that Siri has been set up correctly. Tap *Continue*.

- The iPhone 8 Series (iPhone 8 plus) display alters the color balance to help make the screen show up naturally under distinctive light conditions. You can switch this off in the screen settings after the iPhone 8 Series (iPhone 8 plus) has completed configuring it. Tap *continue* to continue with the setup.

- Has your iPhone been restored? Tap begin to

transfer your computer data to your brand-new iPhone 8 Series (iPhone 8 plus).

- You'll be prompted to ensure your brand-new iPhone 8 Series (iPhone 8 plus) has enough charge to avoid the device turning off in the process of downloading applications and information. Tap *OK* to verify this recommendation.

- You would notice a notification show up on your apps to download in the background.

Chapter 9

iPhone Face ID Secret Features

Reduce Alarm Volume and Keep Screen Brightness with Attention Awareness

Because Face ID can show when you're taking a look at your iPhone's screen, it can make your iPhone respond with techniques that produce sense predicated on your attention. You need to ensure that the interest Aware Features option is geared up by pursuing these steps:

- Tap _Setting_s.

- Tap _Face ID & Passcode._

- Type in your _passcode._

- Move the interest Aware Features slider to

ON/Green

When you do this:

- **_When you have an alarm going off_**: and also you go through the screen, the volume of the alarm will automatically lower because the telephone knows it got your attention.

- **_The screen won't dim to save lots of battery_**: Normally, the screen automatically dims after a brief period, if the telephone sees you are looking at the screen, it understands you're utilizing it and that you would like to start to see the screen.

Get Notification Previews Without Notification Center

Normally, viewing full previews of notifications delivered to you by applications requires starting

Notification Center. Not with Face ID. Since Face ID identifies you and unlocks your mobile phone, there is no risk that another person is viewing your private content. Due to that, changing your notification configurations can provide you with full notification previews without starting Notification Center. Here's how:

- Tap *Settings*.

- Touch *Notifications*.

- Touch *Show Previews*.

- Touch When Unlocked

Now, when you get a notification on your lock screen, take a look at your telephone (but don't swipe through to the screen to unlock it). When Face ID identifies you, the notification will raise to show the entire preview.

Autofill Passwords in Browser

The Autofill is your password as it pertains to authorizing payments or unlocking your phone with Face ID. Do you realize you can also utilize it to log into websites in Browser on the iPhone 8?

That is right: if you store your usernames and passwords in Browser to be auto-filled when you come to login screens, Face ID keeps your that data secure and functional only by you. Some tips about what you must do:

- _Save website usernames and passwords in the Browser when you log in to the sites by touching the pop-up menu._

- _Enable Face ID_ to autofill those usernames and

passwords by going to *Settings -> Face ID & Passcode -> enter your passcode -> moving the Browser Autofill slider to On/Green.*

- Visit a website where you have a merchant account preserved in Browser and go directly to the login screen.

- Touch the username or password field.

- Above the Browser keyboard, touch Passwords.

- In the menu that arises from underneath, touch an individual account you want to use.

- When the facial ID icon appears on the screen, position your iPhone 8 to scan that person. When Face ID authenticates you, your security password is added.

- Log in to the website.

Control Which Apps Can Gain access to Face ID

Every app that would require that you sign in would want to use Face ID since it's faster and better. Your real face scans aren't distributed to the applications (Apple converts the facial scan into an *abstract code*, so there is no risk that any applications could steal that info), nevertheless, you might not want every application to have that access to (you can control how many other data applications can gain access too). If not, here's how to regulate which apps gain access to Face ID:

- Tap *Settings.*

- Touch *Face ID & Passcode.*

- Get into your passcode.

- Tap Other Apps

This screen lists all the applications installed on your iPhone that are looking to use Face ID. To stop apps from being able to access it, move the slider next to these to Off/white.

Switch OFF Face ID Quickly with Buttons

If you're in times where you come to mind that you may be required to use Face ID to unlock your mobile phone and reveal your data-for instance, during a conversation with the authorities or when crossing country borders-you may choose to switch off Face ID. And if time is vital in these circumstances, you would want to do it fast. Listed below are two ways to carefully turn off Face ID by pressing control keys on the iPhone 8:

- At the same time, press and contain the side button on the right of the telephone and either volume button (or both, if you like. Either works); this goes to the Shut down/Emergency screen. Face ID is currently off and also to unlock the telephone; you would be prompted to enter your passcode.

- Press the medial side button five times in quick succession; this causes the Emergency SOS feature, which brings extremely loud siren audio with it, so be ready for that. Touch Cancel on the Emergency SOS screen and then touch Stop Calling to get rid of the decision and the siren. Face ID is currently off.

Use Siri to Turn Off Face ID carefully

In addition to all or any the other activities Siri can do, additionally, it may switch off Face ID for you. That is helpful for quickly turning off Face ID in the situations described earlier. You must have _"Hey Siri"_ allowed for this feature to work, but if you need to do, here's what you must do:

- Without unlocking your telephone, tell it, "Hey Siri, whose telephone is this?"

- Siri will screen whatever info they have about you-generally a name, picture, plus some contact information (unless you want to buy even to show this, remove that from the Address Publication). At exactly the same time, Face ID has been disabled.

- Now, to unlock the telephone or to change Face ID on-again, enter your passcode.

Make Face ID Unlock Faster

Feel just like Face ID takes too much time to identify you and unlock your iPhone? You can speed up the procedure by tweaking:

- Touch *Settings*.

- Touch *Face ID & Passcode*.

- Insert your password.

- Move the *Require Attention for Face ID* slider to Off/white

This boosts *Face ID* speed, but it additionally makes your phone less secure. The *Require Attention* ensures that you are looking at the iPhone and also have your eyes open up for Face ID to unlock your mobile phone. By turning it off, things go faster; however, your telephone could be unlocked even if you are asleep, unconscious, or attempting not to adhere to someone wanting to pressure you to unlock your mobile phone. Keep that risk at heart as you select whether to improve the settings.

Improve Face ID Accuracy

If Face ID doesn't recognize you and the passcode screen appears, enter your passcode immediately; when you do this, Face ID requires the checking of that person it didn't authorize. Adding the new check to the initial, it identifies that person from more perspectives and in more situations.

Face ID eventually throws these short-term matches out because they're not the area of the original, authoritative checkout. But, for some time, they help Face ID work a little much better.

If Face ID often does not identify you correctly, you almost certainly want to create it up again with a fresh face check by going through the process: *Configurations -> Face ID & Passcode -> enter your passcode -> Reset Face ID and then manage it again.*

Chapter 10

How to Group Apps on an iPhone

Creating folders on your iPhone is a sensible way to reduce mess on your home screen. Grouping apps collectively can also make it simpler to use your phone - if all your music applications are in the same place, you would not have to be searching through folders or looking at your mobile phone when you wish to utilize them.

How you create folders isn't immediately apparent, but once you understand the secret, it's simple — some tips about what you should know about how to make a folder on your iPhone.

How to Create Folders and Group Apps on the iPhone

- To make a folder, you will need at least two applications to place into the folder. Determine which two you want to use.

- Gently touch and hold one of the applications until all applications on the screen start shaking (this is the same process that you utilize to re-arrange apps).

NOTE: Making folders on the iPhone 6S and 7 Plus, the iPhone 8 and iPhone 8 Plus, and iPhone 11 Pro and iPhone 11 Max, is just a little trickier. That's because the 3D Touchscreen on those models responds differently to different presses on the screen. When you have one particular cell phones, don't press too much or you'll result in a menu or shortcut. Only a light touch and hold will do.

- Pull one of the applications at the top the other. When the first application appears to merge into the second one, take your finger from the screen. Dropping one form into the other creates the folder.

- What goes on next depends upon what version of the iOS you're working with or using.

  ▪ In iOS 7 and higher, the folder and its own recommended name take up the whole screen.

  ▪ In iOS 4-6, you Typically the two applications and a name for the folder in a strip over the screen

- Every folder has a name assigned to it by default (more on this in a moment); nevertheless, you can transform that name by touching the x icon to clear the recommended name and then type the name you want.

- If you wish to add more applications to the folder, touch the wallpaper to close the folder. Then pull more apps into the new folder.

- When you've added all the applications you want and edited the name, click on the Home button on the leading Center of the iPhone as well as your changes would be saved (precisely like when re-arranging icons).

TIPS: *When you have an iPhone x, XS, or newer, there is no Home button to click. Instead, you should tap **Done** on the right part of the screen.*

How Default iPhone Folder Titles Are Suggested

When you initially create a folder, the iPhone assigns a suggested name to it. That name is chosen predicated on the App Store category that the applications in the folder result from; for instance, if the applications result from the Video games category, the recommended name of the folder is Video games. You should use the recommended name or add your own using the instructions in steps above.

How to Edit Folders on Your iPhone

If you have already created a folder on your iPhone, you might edit it by changing the name, adding or removing apps, and more. Here's how:

- To edit a pre-existing folder, touch and contain the folder until it starts to move.

- Touch it another time, and the folder will open up, and its material will fill up the screen.

- You may make the next changes

- Edit the folder's name by tapping on the written text.

- Add more applications by dragging them in.

- Remove applications from the folder by dragging them away.

- Click on the Home button or the Done button to save lots of your changes.

How to Remove Apps From Folders on iPhone

If you wish to remove an application from a folder on your iPhone or iPod touch, follow these steps:

- Touch and contain the folder that you would like to eliminate the application from.

- When the applications and folders start wiggling, remove your finger from the screen.

- Touch the folder you want to eliminate the application.

- Drag the application from the folder and onto the home screen.

- Click on the Home or Done button to save lots of the new set up.

How to Add Folders to the iPhone Dock

The four applications over the bottom of the iPhone reside in what's called the Dock. You can include folders to the dock if you'd like. To achieve that:

- Move one of the applications currently in the dock away by tapping, keeping, and dragging it to the primary section of the home screen.

- Move a folder into the space.

- Press the home or Done button, depending on your iPhone model, to save lots of the change.

How to Delete a Folder on the iPhone

Deleting a folder is comparable to eliminating an app. Some tips about what you must do:

- Pull all the applications from the folder and onto the home screen.

- When you do that, the folder disappears.

- Press the home or Done button to save lots of the change, and you're done.

Chapter 11

How to Create & Use iPhone 8 Shortcuts

How to Put in a Virtual Home Button to the iPhone

In respect to get a virtual Home button configured, you first have to allow the home button itself. Here's how:

- Touch *Settings*.

- Touch *General*.

- Touch *Accessibility*.

- Touch *AssistiveTouch*.

- Move the *AssistiveTouch* slider to On/green. The digital Home button shows up on your screen.

- Position the button anywhere on your screen using drag and drop.

- Make the button pretty much transparent utilizing the Idle Opacity slider.

- Touch the button to see its default menu.

How to Customize the Virtual Home Button Menu

To change the number of shortcuts and the precise ones that exist in the default menu:

- Around the *Assistive Touch* screen, tap Customize Top Level Menu.

- Change the number of icons shown in the very best Level Menu with the plus and minus control keys at the bottom of the screen. The minimum volume of options is 1; the utmost is 8. Each icon represents a different shortcut.

- To improve a shortcut, touch the icon you want to improve.

- Tap one of the available shortcuts from the list that appears.

- Touch Done to save the change. It replaces the shortcut you have chosen.

- If you decide you want to return to the default group of options, touch Reset.

How to Add Custom Activities to the Virtual Home Button

Now that you understand how to include the virtual Home button and configure the menu, it is time to get to the nice stuff: custom shortcuts. As being a physical Home button, the digital button can be configured to react differently based on how you touch it. Some tips about what you must do:

Within the *AssistiveTouch* screen, go directly to the Custom Actions section. For that section, touch the action that you would like to use to result in the new shortcut. Your alternatives are:

- **Single-Touch**: The original single click of the home button. In cases like this, it's an individual touch on the digital button.

- **Double-Touch**: Two quick touches on the button; if you choose this, you can also control the Timeout establishing (i.e., the time allowed between touches) if additional time goes by between touches, the iPhone goodies them as two solitary touches, not a double-touch.

- *Long Press*: Touch and contain the virtual Home button. If you choose this, you can also configure a Duration, which sets how long you will need to press the screen because of this feature to be triggered.

- *3D Touch*: The 3D Touch screen on modern iPhones lets the screen respond differently based on how hard you press it. Utilize this option to have the digital Home button react to hard presses.

Whichever action you touch, each screen presents several options for shortcuts that you can assign to the action. They are especially cool because they change actions that may normally require pressing multiple control keys into an individual touch.

Most shortcuts are self-explanatory, such as Siri, Screenshot, or Volume Up, but a few need description:

- *Convenience Shortcut*: This shortcut may be used to cause all types of convenience features, such as inverting colors for users with eyesight impairment, turning on VoiceOver, and zooming in on the screen.

- *Shaking*: Choose this, and the iPhone responds to a button touch as if an individual shook the telephone. Shake pays for undoing certain activities, particularly if physical issues prevent you from shaking the telephone.

- *Pinch*: Performs the same as a pinch gesture on the iPhone's screen, which pays for people who've impairments that produce pinching hard or impossible.

- *SOS*: This button allows the iPhone's Emergency

SOS feature, which causes a loud sound to alert others that you might need help and a call to Emergency services.

- *Analytics*: This feature starts the gathering of Assistive Touch diagnostics.

Chapter 12

Useful iPhone 8 Tips & Tricks

Control Your Apple TV With iPhone 8

The Control Focus on the iPhone 8 has an awesome trick: it enables you to regulate your Apple TV if you have one. So long as your iPhone 8 and Apple Television are on a single cellular network, it'll work. Get into Control Center and then look for the Apple Television button that shows up. Touch it and start managing your Apple Television.

How to Enable USB Limited Setting on iPhone 8

Apple just built a robust new security feature into the iPhone 8 with the latest version of iOS; this launch is what's known as *USB Limited Setting* to the iPhone 8.

Lately, companies have been making devices that may be connected to an iPhone's USB slot and crack an iPhone's passcode.

To protect from this, Apple has introduced a USB Restricted Setting. USB Restricted Setting disabled data writing between an iPhone and a USB device if the iPhone is not unlocked to get more than one hour; this effectively makes the iPhone breaking boxes ineffective as they may take hours or times to unlock a locked iPhone.

By default, **USB Limited Mode** is enabled in iOS. But for those who want to disable it, or make sure it hasn't been disabled, go to the *Configurations app* and touch *Face ID & Passcode*. Enter your passcode and then swipe down until you visit a section entitled *"Allow Access When Locked."*

The final toggle in this section is a field that says *"USB Accessories."* The toggle next to them should be turned OFF (white); this implies *USB Restricted Setting* is allowed, and devices can't download or upload data from/to your iPhone if the iPhone is not unlocked to get more than one hour.

Use Two Pane Scenery View

This tip only pertains to the iPhone 8 Pro Max but is cool nonetheless. If you keep your XS device horizontally when using specific applications, you'll see lots of the built-in apps changes to a two-pane setting, including Email and Records. This setting is the main one you observe on an iPad where, for example, you can see a list of all of your records in the Records app while positively reading or editing a single note.

How to stop iPhone 8 Alarms with Your Face

An extremely cool feature of the iPhone 8 is Face ID. It gives you to unlock your phone just by taking a look at it. Face ID also has various other cool features-like that one. Whenever your iPhone 8 or XS security alarm goes off, you could silent it by just picking right up your iPhone and taking a look at it; this tells your iPhone you understand about the arm, and it'll quiet it.

Quickly Disable Face ID

Depending on your geographical area, the police might be able to legally demand you uncover your smartphone at that moment via its facial recognition features. For reasons unknown, facial biometrics aren't protected in the manner fingerprints, and passcodes are; in a few localities. That's why Apple has generated an attribute that lets you quickly disable Face ID in a pinch without going into your settings. Just press the side button five times, and Face ID will be disabled, and you'll need to enter your passcode instead to gain access to your phone.

How decelerate the two times click necessary for Apple Pay

Given that the iPhone 8 jettisoned the Touch ID sensor, you confirm your *Apple Pay* obligations by using Face ID and twice pressing the medial side button. By default, you would need to dual press the medial side button pretty quickly-but it is possible to make things slow down.

To take action, go to *Settings > General > Availability.* Now scroll right down to Side Button. Privately Button screen, you can select between *default, gradual, or slowest*. Pick the speed that is most effective for you.

Chapter 13

How to Fix Common iPhone 8 Problems

iPhone 8 Touch Screen Issues

The bright, beautiful *"edge-to-edge"* OLED screen on the iPhone is one of its major new features; however, the touch screen may sometimes go wrong. Both most common situations are:

✓ *Non-responsive* *SCREEN* *AND* *"GHOST TOUCHES."*

Some users state that the screen on the iPhone 8 sometimes halts working. In those instances, the screen doesn't react to details or touches. In other situations, the contrary occurs: "ghost details" appear to activate things on the screen even when they don't touch it.

If you are experiencing either of these issues, the reason

is the same: a hardware problem with the touch screen chips and detectors in the iPhone 8; because these problems are the effect of a hardware issue, you can't fix them yourself. Fortunately, Apple knows the problem and offers to repair it. Find out about how to proceed on Apple's web page about the problem.

✓ *FROZEN Screen IN WINTER*

A different type of iPhone 8 screen problem that many people run into would be that the screen freezes up and becomes unresponsive for a couple of seconds when going from a warm spot to a chilly one (such as moving out into a wintery day). The good thing is that this is not a hardware problem, so it is much simpler to fix. Try out these quick DIY fix:

- *Update the iOS*: This issue was set with the iOS

11.1.2 update, so make sure you're operating that version of the operating system or higher.

- *Follow Apple's Cold-Weather Recommendations*: Apple has tips and recommendations for the temperatures to use the iPhone in, it suggests not using it in temperature ranges less than 32 degrees F (0 degrees C). Having your iPhone within your clothes and near to your body, warmth is an excellent, simple fix.

iPhone 8 Loudspeaker Problems

The iPhone is a great multimedia device; however, many users report reduced enjoyment of media on the iPhone 8 credited to speaker problems. Listed below are two of the very most common.

a) SPEAKERS Audio MUFFLED

Speakers whose audio is quiet than they ought to, or whose audio sounds muffled, can frequently be fixed by doing the next:

- *Restart iPhone*: Restarting your iPhone can solve all types of problems, including sound issues.

- *Clean the Speakers*. You might have dirt or other gunk developed on the loudspeakers that are leading to the quietness. Understand how to completely clean iPhone speakers.

- *Check the Case*: If you are using a case with your iPhone, make sure there is nothing stuck between your case and the loudspeaker, like pocket lint, that may be causing the problem.

b) Loudspeaker CRACKLES at high volume

Around the other end of the range, some iPhone 8 users have reported that their speakers make a distressing crackling sound when their volume is too high. If this is going on for you, try the next steps:

- *Restart iPhone*: It might not assist in this case, but it's fast and straightforward so that it never hurts to get one of this restart. You can also get one of these hard reset if you want.

- *Update the OS*: Because the latest version of the iOS also includes the latest bug fixes, make sure you're operating it.

- *Talk with Apple*: Crackling loudspeakers are likely to be always a hardware problem that you can't solve. Get active support from Apple instead.

  Some individuals have encountered problems

using Wi-Fi on the iPhone 8. This probably isn't a concern with the iPhone 8 itself. Much more likely, this has regarding software configurations or your Wi-Fi network. Find out about the complexities and fixes in How exactly to Fix an iPhone That Can't Hook up to Wi-Fi in other recommended books at the end of this book.

iPhone 8 Charging Problems

The iPhone 8 is the first iPhone to add support for wireless charging. That's cool, but it isn't cool if the telephone won't charge properly. If you are facing that problem, try these steps to repair it:

- ***Get one of these New Charging Wire***: Maybe the charging problem has been your wire, not your phone. Try another wire you know for certain works. Make especially certain to either use the official Apple wire or one that's qualified by Apple.

- ***Remove Credit cards From Case***: If you are wanting to charge cellular and have an instance that also stores things such as credit cards, take away the credit cards. The cellular payment top features of the credit cards can hinder the cellular charging.

- ***Remove Case for Wifi Charging***: Removing the whole case may be considered a good idea if you are charging wirelessly. Not absolutely all cases are appropriate for cellular charging, so that they may be avoiding normal function.

- ***Restart iPhone***: You never know very well what types of problems a restart can solve. This may be one of them.

iPhone 8 Electric battery Life Problems

There is nothing worse than not having the ability to use your mobile phone because it's working out of electric battery too early, but that's the thing some users complain about. And with most of its fresh, power-hungry features - the OLED screen, for example - it isn't a shock that there could be some iPhone 8 electric battery problems.

Fortunately, battery issues on the iPhone are simple enough to solve using the settings included in iOS. Below are a few tips:

- *Learn to Preserve Battery*: There are over 30+ tips about how to raise your iPhone's electric battery life. Use a few of these as well as your iPhone would run much longer between charges.

- *Update the OS*: Furthermore, to fix a bug, new variations of iOS often deliver improvements that make the battery better. Install the latest revise, and you'll see your electric battery last longer.

- *Get a protracted Life Electric battery*: Maybe the simplest way to get your electric battery to go longer is to obtain additional battery. There are sorts of prolonged life batteries on the marketplace, from exterior dongles to others.

iPhone 8 Face ID Problems

Most likely, the single coolest feature of the iPhone 8 is the facial ID, the facial recognition system. This feature is utilized for security and convenience: it unlocks the telephone, can be used to enter passwords, and even authorizes Apple Pay transactions. But issues with Face ID and either front or back camera can cause your iPhone

8 never to identify you. If you are (ahem) facing this issue, try these pointers:

- *Adjust iPhone Position*: If Face ID sometimes identifies you, but other times doesn't, consider changing the position you're holding the telephone. As the Face ID sensors are relatively sophisticated, they need to be capable of getting a good view of that person to work.

- *Clean "The Notch."*: THE FACIAL ID detectors are situated in "the notch," the deep cut-out near the top of the screen. If those receptors get protected with dirt or even enough oil from your skin layer, their standard procedure could be reduced. Try wiping "the notch" clean.

- *Update the OS*: Apple regularly enhances the

speed and precision of Face ID, as well as fixes insects, in new variations of the iOS. If you are having Face ID problems on iPhone 8, make sure you're using the latest operating system.

- *Reset Face ID*: The problem is probably not with Face ID itself, but instead with the initial scans of that person created when you set up Face ID to start. If the other activities haven't helped, be rid of your old face scans and make new ones. Enter a shiny, well-lit place and then go to Configurations -> Face ID & Passcode -> enter your passcode -> Reset Face ID. Then create Face ID from scratch.

- *Contact Apple*: If none of the things has helped, there may be a problem with the hardware in your iPhone 8 (maybe it's a problem with the video cameras, the Face ID sensors, or another thing). If so, you should contact Apple to obtain an analysis of the problem and a fix.

- *You might have seen tales on the internet claiming that Face ID has been hacked*: They are virtually all bogus. Face ID can be an extremely advanced system that depends on thousands of data factors to identify a face. Yes, similar twins might be able to beat Face ID (it seems sensible; they have simply the same face!). Other families that look nearly the same as one another can also be able to technique it. But also, for the most part, the probability of Face ID being tricked or hacked is very, surprisingly low.

iPhone 8 Screen Issues

The iPhone 8 was the first iPhone to use the brighter, better OLED screen technology. The screen appears excellent, but it's susceptible to some issues that other iPhones using different systems aren't. Perhaps most obviously among these is "burn off in."; this happens when the same image is shown on a screen for an extended period, resulting in faint "spirits" of these images showing up on the screen regularly, regardless of what else has been screened. Fortunately, OLED burn-in is simple to avoid. Just follow these pointers:

- *Lower Screen Lighting*: The low the lighting of your screen, the less likely a graphic burn off involved with it. You have two options here. First, you can by hand reduce your screen brightness by starting Control Center and moving the lighting slider down. On the other hand, let your screen brightness change to ambient light by heading to *Configurations -> General -> Convenience -> Screen brightness -> Auto-Brightness.*

- *Set Screen to Auto-Lock*: Burn off happens when a graphic is on the screen for an extended period. So, if your screen hair and shuts off regularly, the image can't burn off. Set your screen to lock by heading to Configurations automatically -> Screen & Lighting -> Auto-Lock and choose five minutes or less.

Another screen problem that impacts some iPhone 8 models is a green line that appears at the right edge of the screen. That is another hardware problem that users can't fix themselves. If you see this, your very best wager is to get hold of Apple to get active support.

Chapter 14

iPhone 8 Gestures You Should Know

Just like the iPhone 7 launched in 2017, the iPhone 8 doesn't include a physical home button, instead deciding on gestures to regulate the new user interface. It would require a couple of days to get used to the change but stay with it. By day three, you'll question how you ever coped without it, and using an "old" iPhone would appear old and antiquated.

1. **<u>Unlock your iPhone 8</u>:** Go through the phone and swipe up from underneath the screen. It truly is that easy, and also you don't need to hold back for the padlock icon at the very top to improve to the unlock visual before swiping up.

2. **<u>Touch to wake</u>:** Tap on your iPhone 8 screen

when it's off to wake it up and find out what notifications you have. To unlock it with FaceID, you'll still have to set it up.

3. **<u>Back to the Homescreen</u>:** Whatever application you are in, if you would like to return to the Home screen, swipe up from underneath of the screen. If you're within an application that is operating scenery, you'll need to keep in mind slipping up from underneath the screen (i.e., the medial side) rather than where, in fact, the Home button used to be.

4. **<u>Have a screenshot</u>:** Press the power button and the volume up button together quickly, and it would snap a screenshot of whatever is on the screen.

5. **Addressing Control Centre:** It used to be always a swipe up, now it's a swipe down from the very best right of the screen. Even if your iPhone doesn't have 3D Touch, you can still long-press on the symbols to gain usage of further configurations within each icon.

6. **Accessing open up apps:** Previously you raise tapped on the home button to uncover what apps you'd open. You now swipe up and then pause with your finger on the screen. After that, you can see the applications you have opened up in the order you opened them.

7. **Launch Siri:** When you may use the "Hey Siri" hot term to awaken Apple's digital associate, there are still ways to release the function utilizing a button press. Press and contain the wake/rest

button on the right aspect of the phone before Siri interface pops-up on screen.

8. **<u>Switch your phone off</u>**: Because long-pressing the wake/rest button launches Siri now, there's a fresh way for switching the phone off. To take action, you would need to press and contain the wake/rest button and the volume down button at the same time. Now glide to power off.

9. **<u>Release Apple Pay</u>**: Again, the wake/rest button is the main element here. Double touch it, and it would talk about your Apple Budget, then scan that person, and it'll request you to keep your phone near to the payment machine.

10. **<u>Gain access to widgets on the lock screen</u>**: Swipe from still left to directly on your lock screen, ideal

for checking your activity bands.

Using Memoji

- **<u>Create your Memoji</u>:** Open up Messages and begin a new meaning. Touch the tiny monkey icon above the keypad, and then strike the "+" button to generate your personality. You would customize face form, skin tone, curly hair colour, eye, jewelry, plus much more.

- **<u>Use your Memoji/Animoji in a FaceTime call</u>:** Take up a FaceTime call, then press the tiny star icon underneath the corner. Now, tap the Memoji you want to use.

- **<u>Memoji your selfies</u>:** So, if you select your Memoji face, preferably to your real to life face, you can send selfies with the Memoji changing your head in Messages. Take up a new message and touch the camera icon, and then press that top button. Now choose the Animoji option by tapping that monkey's mind again. Choose your Memoji and tap the 'x,' not the "done" button, and then take your picture.

- **<u>Record a Memoji video</u>**: Sadly, Memoji isn't available as a choice in the camera app, but that doesn't mean you can't record one. Much like the picture selfie, go to communications, touch on the camera icon and then slip to video and then tap on the superstar. Weight the Animoji or your Memoji, and off you decide to go.

iOS 13 iPhone 8 Notification Tips

- *Notifications collection to provide quietly*: If you're worried that you would be getting way too many notifications, you can place the way they deliver with an app by application basis. Swipe left when you've got a notification on the Lock screen and touch on Manage. Touch Deliver Quietly. Calm notifications come in Notification Centre, but do not show up on the Lock screen, play audio, present a banner or badge the application icon. You've just surely got to be sure you check every once in a while.

- *Switch off notifications from an app*: Same method as the "Deliver Quietly" feature, other than you tap the "Switch off..." option.

- *Open up Notification Centre on Lock screen*: From your lock screen, swipe up from the center of the screen, and you would visit a long set of earlier notifications if you have any.

- *Check Notifications anytime*: To check on your Notifications anytime, swipe down from the very best left part of the screen to reveal them.

Using Screen Time

- *Checking your Screen Time*: You can examine how you've been making use of your phone with the new Screen Time feature in iOS 13. You'll find the reviews in *Configurations > Screen Time.*

- *Scheduled Downtime:* If you want just a little help making use of your mobile phone less, you can restrict what applications you utilize when. Check out Settings > Screen Time and choose the Downtime option. Toggle the change to the "on" position and choose to routine a period when only specific applications and calls are allowed. It's ideal for preventing you or your children from using their cell phones after an arranged time, for example.

- ***Set application limits***: App Limitations enable you to choose which group of applications you want to include a period limit to. Choose the category and then "add" before choosing a period limit and striking "plans."

- ***Choose "always allowed" apps***: However, you might be willing to lock down your phone to avoid you utilizing it, that's no good if most of your way of getting in touch with people is via an application that gets locked away. Utilize this feature always to allow certain applications whatever limitations you apply.

- **_Content & Personal privacy limitations_**: This section is also within the primary Screen Time configurations menu and particularly useful if you are a mother or father with kids who use iOS devices. Utilizing it, you can restrict all types of content and options, including iTunes and in-app buys, location services, advertising, etc. It's worth looking at.

Siri shortcuts

- **_Siri Shortcuts_**: There are several little "help" the iPhone 8 offers via Siri Shortcuts. To start to see the ones recommended for you, go to *Configurations > Siri & Search* and choose what you think would be helpful from the automatically produced suggestions. Touch "all shortcuts" to see more. If you wish to install specific "shortcuts" for a variety of different applications that aren't recommended by the iPhone, you can do this by downloading the dedicated Siri Shortcuts.

iPhone 8 Control Centre Tips

- *Add new handles*: Just like the previous version of iOS, you can include and remove handles from Control Centre. Check out *Configurations > Control Centre > Customise Handles* and then choose which settings you would like to add.

- *Reorganize handles*: To improve the order of these settings, you've added, touch, and contain the three-bar menu on the right of whichever control you would like to move, then move it along the list to wherever you would like it to be.

- *Expand handles*: Some settings may become full screen, press harder on the control you want to expand, and it will fill the screen.

- *Activate screen recording*: Among the new options, you can include regulating Centre is Screen Recording. Be sure you add the control, then open up Control Centre and press the icon that appears like an excellent white circle in the thin white band. To any extent further, it'll record everything that occurs on your screen. Press the control again if you are done, and it will save a video to your Photos application automatically.

- ***Adjust light/screen brightness***: You can activate your camera adobe flash, utilizing it as a torch by starting Control Centre and tapping on the torch icon. If you wish to adjust the lighting, power press the icon, then adapt the full-screen slider that shows up.

- ***Quickly switch where a sound is played***: One cool feature is the capability to change where music is playing. While music is playing, through Apple Music, Spotify, or wherever, press on the music control or touch the tiny icon in the very best part of the music control; this introduces a pop-up screening available devices that you can play through; this may be linked earphones, a Bluetooth loudspeaker, Apple Television, your iPhone, or any AirPlay device.

- ***Set an instant timer***: Rather than going to the timer app, you can force press on the timer icon, then glide up or down on the full-screen to create a timer from about a minute to two hours long.

- ***How to gain access to HomeKit devices***: Open up Control Center and then tap on the tiny icon that appears like a home.

iPhone 8 Photos and Camera Tips

- ***Enable/disable Smart HDR***: Among the new iPhone's camera advancements is HDR, which helps boost colors, light, and detail in hard light conditions. It's on by default, but if you would like to get it turned on or off, you manually can check out *Settings > Camera and discover the Smart HDR toggle change.*

- ***Keep a standard photograph with HDR***: Right under the Smart HDR toggle is a "Keep Normal Photo" option, which would save a regular, no HDR version of your picture as well as the Smart HDR photo.

- ***Portrait Lights***: To take Portrait Setting shots with artificial lights, first go to capture in Family portrait mode. Portrait Setting only works for people on the iPhone 8 when capturing with the rear-facing camera. To choose your Portrait Setting capturing style, press and hang on the screen where it says "DAYLIGHT" and then move your finger to the right.

- *Edit Portrait Lights after taking pictures*: Open up any Family portrait shot in Photos and then tap "edit." After another or two, you will see the light effect icon at the bottom of the image, touch it, and swipe just as you did when shooting the image.

- *Edit Portrait setting Depth*: Using the new iPhone 8, you can modify the blur impact after shooting the Portrait shot. Check out Photos and choose the picture you want to regulate, then select "edit." You will see a depth slider at the bottom of the screen. Swipe to boost the blur strength, swipe left to diminish it.

- *How exactly to Merge People in Photos app*: Photos in iOS can check out your photos and identify people and places. If you discover that the application has chosen the same person, but says they vary, you can combine the albums collectively. To get this done, go directly to the Photos application > Albums and choose People & Places. Touch on the term "Select" at the very top right of the screen and then choose the images of individuals you want to merge, then tap "merge."

- **Remove people in Photos app**: Head to Photos App, Albums, and choose People & Places. To eliminate tap on "Choose" and then tap on individuals you do not want to see before tapping on "Remove" underneath still left of your iPhone screen.

iPhone 8: Keyboard Tips

- **Go one-handed**: iOS 13's QuickType keypad

enables you to type one-handed, which is fantastic on the larger devices like the iPhone 8 and XS Greatest extent. Press and contain the emoji or world icon and then keypad configurations. Select either the still left or right-sided keypad. It shrinks the keypad and techniques it to 1 aspect of the screen. Get back to full size by tapping the tiny arrow.

- *Use your keyboard as a trackpad*: Previously, with 3D Touch shows, you utilize the keyboard area as a trackpad to go the cursor on the screen. You'll still can, but it works just a little in a different way here, rather than pressure pressing anywhere on the keypad, press, and hangs on the spacebar instead.

Face ID Tips

- *Adding another in-person ID*: if you regularly change appearance now, you can put in a second In person ID to state the iPhone 8 getting puzzled. That is also really useful if you would like to add your lover to allow them to use your mobile phone while you're traveling, for example.

iPhone 8: Screen Tips

- *Standard or Zoomed screen*: Since iPhone 6 Plus, you've had the opportunity to select from two quality options. You can transform the screen settings from Standard or Zoomed on the iPhone 8 too. To change between your two - if you have changed your mind after set up - go to

Configurations > Screen & Lighting > Screen Focus and choose Standard or Zoomed.

- ***Enable True Tone screen***: If you didn't get it done at the step, you could transform it anytime. To get the iPhone's screen to automatically change its color balance and heat to complement the background light in the area, check out Control Centre and push press the screen lighting slider. Now touch the True Firmness button. You can even go to *Configurations > Screen and Lighting and toggle the "True Shade" switch.*

iPhone 8 Battery Tips

- *Check your average battery consumption*: In iOS 13, you can check out Settings > Battery, and you will see two graphs. One shows the electric battery level; the other shows your screen on and screen off activity. You would find two tabs. One shows your last day; the other turns up to fourteen days; this way, you can view how energetic your phone battery strength and breakdowns screening your average screen on and off times show under the graphs.

- *Enable Low-Power Mode*: The reduced Power Mode (Settings > Electric battery) enables you to reduce power consumption. The feature disables or reduces history application refresh, auto-downloads, email fetch, and more (when allowed). You can turn it on at any point, or you are prompted to carefully turn it on at the 20 and 10 % notification markers. You can even put in control to regulate Centre and get access to it quickly by swiping up to gain access to Control Center and tapping on the electric battery icon.

- *Find electric battery guzzling apps*: iOS specifically lets you know which apps are employing the most power. Head to Configurations > Electric battery and then scroll right down to the section that provides you an in-depth look at all of your battery-guzzling apps.

- *Check your battery via the Electric battery widget*: Inside the widgets in Today's view, some cards enable you to start to see the battery life staying in your iPhone, Apple Watch, and linked headphones. Just swipe from left to directly on your Home screen to access your Today view and scroll until you start to see the "Batteries" widget.

- *Charge wirelessly*: To utilize the iPhone's wifi charging capabilities, buy a radio charger. Any Qi charger will continue to work, but to charge more effectively, you will need one optimized for Apple's 7.5W charging.

- *Fast charge it*: When you have a 29W, 61W, or 87W USB Type-C power adapter for a MacBook, you can plug in your iPhone 8 Pro utilizing a Type-C to Lightning wire watching it charge quickly. Up to 50 % in thirty minutes.

Chapter 15

5 Ways of Upgrading Your iPhone Digital Photography for Instagram

1. Minimalism is Key

Our number 1 Instagram photography suggestion is to consider photos that look great and professional with your iPhone; you would need to believe. Why? Because it is not only better - but it's much simpler to choose one exciting subject matter and make that the center point of your image.

The sure sign of the amateur is a person who tries to match so many subjects to their imagery. "But my image would be filled with vacant space!" you may protest. That's flawlessly fine. Professional photographers call bare space, *'negative space'*, which is another technique which makes your center point stand out.

The ultimate way to do this is to go closer to the topic and remove anything in the shot that may distract the viewer.

This can make your Instagram photography appear to be like it was done by an expert. As you keep up to apply this, you'll come to find that minimalism is the most shared on systems like Instagram, because photos with ONE center point stick out on smartphone screens.

2. **Get low in Position**

Understandably, your camera move shouldn't be filled with selfies. Just as your camera move shouldn't contain images used at chest elevation.

Among the quickest ways to update your Instagram digital photography and create images that stick out is to take from a lesser position than what you're used to. You don't need to get too low either, capture from less than what you're used to.

When you take your subject or centre point from such a minimal angle that the sky is the only background, what you finish up doing is following both Instagram picture taking Tip 1 and Tip 2 - making the image extremely attractive on the system like Instagram.

So when you're finally more comfortable with the thought of looking, "extra" according to some people, you'll be able to start squatting and even kneeling to be able to get the best low-angle images.

3. <u>Depth of Field</u>

Exactly what does *"depth of field"* mean? Blurring backgrounds, of course! Everyone knows an image with blur looks a lot more interesting than a graphic where the background and the foreground are both in concentration.

When you utilize zoom lens accessories to mention a feeling of depth in your images, i.e. Telephoto lenses, you'll be able to attract people's attention - whether you're photographing accessories for Instagram, or just taking a scenery photograph.

Besides getting hold of iPhone accessories, a straightforward technique like using "leading lines" that direct the audiences' focus on whatever it is that has been photographed is a superb way to produce depth for your Instagram digital photography. For instance, going for a picture of the road, railway track, a riverbank, fences, and pathways are an excellent leading line!

Once you have found your leads, you can create some depth in the foreground by using found items like stones or leaves or other things, for example, When you absolutely cannot find anything in the foreground that could add a component appealing, then get back to Suggestion #2 and "Get Low in position"! Take from a lesser angle, and you will be amazed what you can catch.

4. <u>Get Up-Close and Personal</u>

Okay, so right now, you've probably determined that each of the tips accumulates from the prior tips so that by enough time you've mastered this whole list, you're practically an expert!

Your Instagram picture taking needs details! It might be hard to trust, but a great deal of iPhone professional photographers make the error of not getting close enough to the centre point. Particularly when they're photographing something with a great deal of fine detail - i.e. When you capture from a long distance, the picture eventually ends up being a little dull and impersonal; however, when you get near to the thing, you all of a sudden have an image that involves life - particularly when you take portraits of others or even your selfies. When you move nearer to the subject, you can properly catch cosmetic features and feelings that would build relationships with the viewer.

Even the newer iPhones remain unable to shoot HQ images of subject matter close up and personal, so our reward Instagram photography suggestion is that you would have to get your hands on the macro zoom lens, like the *TrueLux macro zoom lens*.

What this zoom lens can do is allow your camera to target incredibly near to whatever you're shooting and then add visual interest (and depth) to your photograph, simultaneously.

5. Don't Be Scared of the Silhouette

That one seems just like a no-brainer, but many individuals continue to be afraid to embrace silhouettes on the Instagram grid.

First of all, *what is a silhouette? It's mostly when an object's form is captured against a gleaming light. It's not the same thing as a shadow.*

Silhouettes add an air of secret to an image, and against

an extremely bright background, a silhouette really can look quite beautiful on your Instagram feed!

Another best part concerning this particular Instagram photography technique is that it is really simple to create images of a silhouette on your iPhone. You just need to know what you want to take a picture of, and then capture towards the light. That's it!

If you'd like to ensure that your subject's silhouette looks unmistakable but still dark, check out your iPhone camera app, tap the screen to create the focus, and then swipe right down to darken the camera exposure - you can still darken the subject even further with photography editing apps.

The optimum time to consider silhouette photographs, despite having your iPhone, is during what professional photographers refer to as the *golden hours of sunrise and sunset.* When sunlight is low coming, then you can position the source of light behind the topic, which means that you'll get a perfectly coloured sky as the backdrop - taking benefit of tips 1 to 4.

You do not necessarily have to hold back for the golden hour to consider silhouette photographs, so long as your source of light is behind the subject.

For instance, if you are shooting indoors, you merely have to put your subject before the window (to consider advantage of daylight), or before a band light/ softbox if daylight is no option.

CHAPTER 16

Hot Tips & Methods to take Pleasure from more Features

Here are some guidelines to help you love the more exceptional features on your iPhone.

How to Use Two Apps simultaneously with Slide Over & Break up View

Do you want to manage your calendar or any other even while you are checking your Email? No issue, this section will show you how.

Need to research something online by safari without dropping off your gained access to on iBooks or any other? Now it's easy!

Slide Over allows you to quickly use the other App without terminating the first (or departing the display) and **SPLIT UP View** will enable you to use two Apps on the display screen simultaneously - forget about needing to interchange laterally!

How to Swiftly Use another App with Slide Over

In my instance, I've safari opened up on the screen, and I have to check something on the calendar:

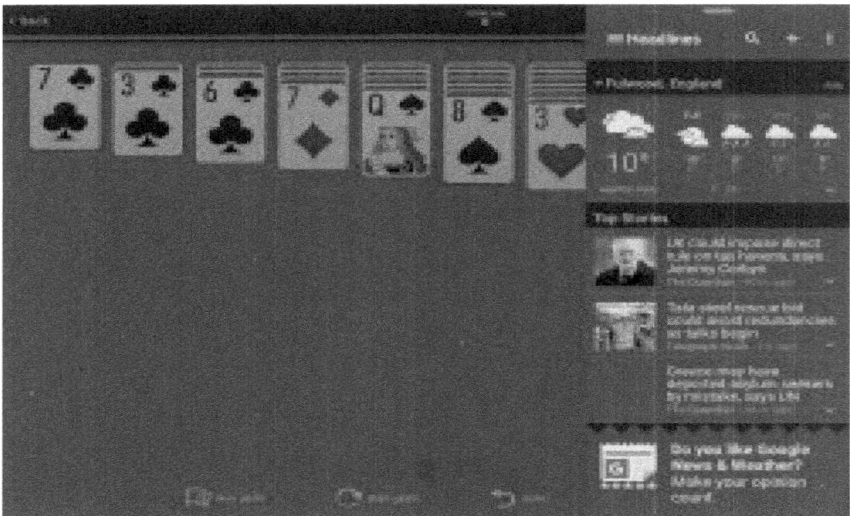

- Together with your first App open up on the screen, SWIPE in from the right-hand advantage of the display to open up **SLIDE OVER**.

- This will open up a panel running the ultimate App you used (previous in the primary windows). To alternative, this to a distinctive or new App, pull down the tiny gray pub from the very best of the Slip Over -panel. The App in the primary windowpane will dim into the background.

- Please scroll through the set of Apps to find the main one you want to open up and Tap it to open it up in slip over.

- Together with your chosen App opened up, you might now utilize it as if it's been on the original main display screen. To disregard it and go again to your earlier App, swipe the other App to the right-hand corner of the screen.

How to Use Two Apps Side-by-Side with Break up View

Having opened the next App with a slip over as instructed above, switching to a split view can be more comfortable.

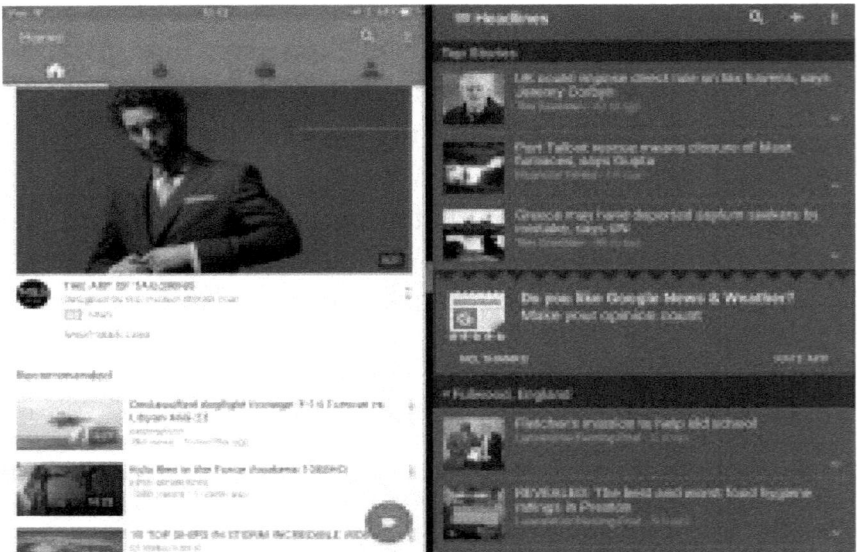

- With another App opened up in slip over, swipe the white pub toward the center of the screen. The dimmed down Background App will brighten again, which indicates that glide over has turned into the split up view. Each App is usable, impartial of each other.

- To improve the other App, swipe the grey pub down from the very best of the screen and select a distinctive App from the list. To close a divided view, pull the divider to the right-hand side of the screen.

As you observe, using split view can be a development of Slip Over, and helps it be easy to "get things achieved" without the difficulty of continually turning back and forth between two Apps. The power of the iPhone method is that you will have the capacity of using high-performance Apps side-by-side without it lacking a defeat, that's brilliant if you get a Face Time Video Call if you are in the center of editing an image!

How to Manage Notifications

Notifications are your device's way of letting you know what's occurring in an App. This may be information including a note or Email notification, on every occasion you install an App; it'll have its pre-decided configurations about just how it interacts with you (via notifications); nevertheless, you could easily change them, or forestall notifications from happening at all.

Lock display notifications on the iPhone will come in two primary forms, banners and Notifications. Banners Appear near the top of the display screen, and Notifications which shows up at the guts of the lock screen. Probably the most glaring difference when working with your iPhone is that banners vanish automatically after a couple of seconds; however, notification alert needs an action brought on (typically only a select) before they disappear.

Your iPhone has notification middle; which shows you all the notifications you have obtained within the last 24 hours, that you haven't already taken action on - If you **OKAY** an alert for example, then it will not show in the notification middle.

Gain access to the iPhone Notification Centre

Swipe down from the very best side of the iPhone screen, and you will see two headings near the top of the screen notifications.

Follow the below process to gain access to the notification middle;

- "Today" gives you an accurate overview of your programs for your day - the weather, any calendar entries, and almost every other things you've gained access to. You might scroll to the low part and edit the Apps that could show information there.

- "Notifications" shows all information from the previous day that you have previously used. All Apps that generate notifications is seen in this list if you don't choose to exclude them (I will display for you ways to do this below).

- Tapping on any notification upon this list will need you to the little bit of information in the App that produced it - Tapping on the tweets notification, for example, would open up the tweets App which specific tweet.

- To clear notifications from confirmed App, select the x at the right-hand part of its name bar, then Tap **CLEAR**. There isn't any clear all function, lamentably, so you will want to achieve that for each App in the list to vacant the list.

How to Change an App's Notification Preferences

Every App gets the same simple configurations as long as notifications are concerned.

- From the home display, find and select **SETTINGS**.

- In the primary settings menu, Tap **NOTIFICATIONS**.

- At the very top, you might see options showing the order where notifications are shown within the notification center. You can transform this by

Tapping on this and choosing almost every other option. Below this, you will notice a summary of every one of the Apps on your iPhone, and beneath their name, you will see their notification options. To edit a credit card application options, Tap its Name.

- You may locate switches to regulate whether to allow Notifications if to show on Lock Display or in the Notification Centre and various options. You can additionally select if notifications should show as Banners or Notifications when the iPhone is unlocked, or by no means, by Tapping the right choice.

While you're pleased with your configuration for the App, Tapping the blue arrow at the very top left-hand corner will lead you back to the menu, helping you to edit various other App's configurations.

Quick actions from Notifications

If you get a text message or email even while you're utilizing your iPhone, you'll get a banner notification that shows near the top of the screen. You may get off this by swiping it upwards to continue using what you're doing. However, if you swipe it downwards, you'll access three other available choices.

Swiping downwards on the text notification will show the keyboard, letting you instantly answer the message and never have to change application. Swiping down on a contact notification gives you the decision of replying to or deleting the e-mail.

Around the lock display screen, you could additionally swipe from left on a contact notification to send it right to garbage without even unlocking your iPhone.

How to Update the iPhone Operating System (iOS Version)

Under normal circumstances, the operating-system of your iPhone called **iOS** (*iPhone Operating-System*) would look for updates itself, and also bring to your notice when the first is available by putting a red badge on the configurations icon. It will not set up itself though; you will do that!

To set up an update to iOS, follow the below steps:

- At the home screen, locate and select on **SETTINGS**.

- Inside the settings menu, Tap **GENERAL**.

- Tap on **COMPUTER SOFTWARE UPDATE**.

If the phone is current, you will see a message on-screen letting you know so. When there is any upgrade available, information for this will be shown on-screen together with a setup prompt as a means to begin the revise. You can likewise consent to new terms & conditions for the working device too!

Your phone may restart several time later during the update process, and also you may not have the ability of utilizing it as it's updating. So; it is best to set up an update on your phone when you understand you're not in all probability to need it within the timeframe the update would maintain progress!